Contemporary Indian Society

About the Editors

Dr. Jyoti Prasad Saikia is currently a Professor in the Department of Sociology, Dibrugarh University. He is working in the field of Gender Studies. He has written and edited a number of books. Among these, 'Gender & Health: A Sociological Insight', 'Gender: Themes & Issues', 'Youth and Career Aspiration', 'Problems of Education in Rural Women', 'Gender Trouble: A Study in North East India' and 'Flash From North-East India' are significant.

Dr. Shweta Prasad is currently an Associate Professor at the Department of Sociology, Faculty of Social Sciences, Banaras Hindu University, Varanasi. She is also the Convener of the RC 10 (Research Committee on Gender Studies) of the Indian Sociological Society. She has been a UGC-Research Awardee (2014-16) and has received the "Leadership Training Award for Asian Women in Agriculture R&D" by the International Rice Research Institute, Philippines. She has completed an international project in collaboration with the IRRI, Philippines along with a major research project funded by UGC. She has also authored two books. Her areas of interest are Women and Globalization, Corporate Social Responsibility and Women Empowerment, Violence against Women and Employment/impoverishment of Women due to the application of new agricultural technologies.

Contemporary Indian Society

A Gendered Perspective

Edited by

Jyoti Prasad Saikia
Shweta Prasad

CONCEPT PUBLISHING COMPANY PVT. LTD.,
NEW DELHI-110059

ISBN-13: 978-93-5125-285-6

First Published 2017

Published and Printed by

Concept
Since 1974

Concept Publishing Company Pvt. Ltd.
Regd. Office:
A/15-16, Commercial Block, Mohan Garden,
New Delhi-110059 (INDIA)
Phones : 25351460, 25351794, *Fax* : 091-11-25357109
Email : publishing@conceptpub.com
Website: www.conceptpub.com

Cataloging in Publication Data--Courtesy: D.K. Agencies (P) Ltd. <docinfo@dkagencies.com>

Contemporary Indian society : a gendered perspective / edited by Jyoti Prasad Saikia, Shweta Prasad.
pages cm
Includes bibliographical references and index.
ISBN 9789351252856

1. Women—India—Social conditions. 2. Sex discrimination against women—India. I. Saikia, Jyoti Prasad, editor. II. Prasad, Shweta, editor.

HQ1742.C66 2017 DDC 305.40954 23

**Dedicated to those
who are engaged in the quest for
ensuring equality and equity for
Women in India**

काशी हिन्दू विश्वविद्यालय
BANARAS HINDU UNIVERSITY
An Institution of National Importance established by an Act of Parliament

प्रो. गिरीश चन्द्र त्रिपाठी
कुलपति
Prof. Girish Chandra Tripathi
Vice-Chancellor

Varanasi-221005 (INDIA)
Phone : 91-542-2368939, 2368339
Fax : 91-542-2369100, 2369951
E-mail : vc@bhu.ac.in
Website : www.bhu.ac.in

Foreword

Gender, being an integral part of human existence and experience, plays a crucial role in the development of persona and their survival tactics for improving the quality of life. Thus, gender has gradually evolved as a significant issue in the discourses on society and social issues. But it has so far focussed, primarily on women. Men and trans-genders have found very little attention in the gender space.

The contemporary Indian women, even without formal educational qualifications, have huge exposures. Hence, they are continuously striving to break their stereo typed roles. As the awareness and prosperity rises and education percolates within the society, newer kinds of deprivations and marginalisation issues are being brought out, seeking due attention.

The book "Contemporary Indian Society: A Gendered Perspective" is a serious effort to assimilate the multi dimensional researches being carried out by the scholars on gender studies. The volume reports works from Jammu to Bengaluru and Gujarat to Assam, covering whole India geographically. The book compactly covers the issues of individuality and development, portrayal in media, gender equality, gendering of family planning, status of working women after various governmental legislative interventions, rights of underprivileged sector of the society specially women and work associated economic empowerment but relative deprivation due to gender disparity. The issues of witch hunting and its inherent politics for disenfranchising women's control over her resources are also well elaborated.

I see in Gender Studies, a possibility to provide a matured understanding of the social relations that exists that if improved can help women harness their full potential. This would then facilitate them to contribute meaningfully to the national growth and in turn improvise their own quality of life.

I congratulate the authors and the editors for ably portraying the challenges within the survival-ecology of the today's women in India, and the understanding of the myriad restrictions in fulfilment of their aspirations.

Girish Chandra Tripathi

Contents

Introduction

The study of gender has occupied an important place in the discourse of sociology in a new era, and its area has been increasing in every nook and corner of the world. Today a keen desire for studying gender related issues and phenomenon has rapidly expanded to both the students and researchers. At the same time, it raises a question on the perspective of studying the gender related issues from sociological point of views. Can we continue gender studies as the study of women only? Indeed, we should be aware of the fact that gender is related to masculinity and feminity instead of male and female. However, gender is biologically constructed, which cannot be solely intermixed with sex. Of course, a debate on sex-gender has been continued till today. Besides, male and female, the gender studies include transgenders also. However, we feel that gender should be considered an integral part of all human experiences. As gender plays a key role of family habits, choices and life-styles of every human life, it is very idea of studying the relevance of gender in various perspectives across the limitations of time and space.

This book includes the studies of some important issues relating to gender. They want to highlight the role and status, justice and plight of women in a male dominated society. The first chapter entitled, "Gender Studies and its Significance in Contemporary Society" by Dola Borkataki highlights the reasons why we have observed an unprecedented rise in the interest of researchers all over the world towards gender related issues and the significance of the same in today's society.

Arvinder A. Ansari's contribution on, "Minority Within Minority: Understanding Muslim Women's Activism in India" highlights the condition of Muslim women in a patriarchal society. The chapter also focuses upon the constant negation women undergo in regard to the personal and the political or the tussle between their private self and the public domain. Ansari has examined the battle still being waged by India's Muslim women for their identity and its shortcomings resulting from the failure of Islamic feminist activism to turn into an organized 'social movement'. The study attempts to understand if Muslim women in India are empowered to deny patriarchy, and ignore customary laws and if they can, in what ways. The study explores the position of Muslim women between culture, religion, law and politics and her attempt to make feminist stand. In other words, Ansari is looking at the complex position that Muslim women finds themselves in where they will have to be Muslims and must join the activism to have the freedom they deserve. This study is a beautiful examination of all this intriguing issues.

The chapter, "Gender, Conflict and Violence in Jammu & Kashmir" by Abha Chauhan paints a qualitative picture of the complex interactions of conflict, violence and gender in Jammu & Kashmir. She has focused upon the political activism and social movements, views of women on the violence by armed forces, women's agency in regard to political participation and conflict resolution. Through a gendered analysis of conflict in Jammu & Kashmir the study finds that Women's experiences of conflict and violence are not homogeneous, but contextual and shifting. While women actively supported armed conflict (*tehreek*), the *Mujahids* and even assisted them to cross over the border for arms training and lent all possible help; such support has now declined. Although, women have participated in the political arena, primarily for ending the conflict, they themselves see their activity as non-political and an extension of their domestic concerns. Further, these acts get marginalized when time comes formal politics to take over the negotiations. The study finds that the absence of autonomous and secular women's organizations and groups has limited the space for women's agency.

The study, "Individuality as 'Capability Deprivation': A Critical Analysis in the Context of Women and Development in India" by Hriday Ranjan Kalita and Jyoti Prasad Saikia, has made an attempt to explore the possibility that the kind of individuality that our society allows women to develop may act as a factor lead to 'capability deprivation' in terms of getting the full benefits of 'development' that our nation has to offer today. Although a theoretical study, admittedly limited in its generalizability, it makes a critical enquiry into the question whether the state of 'individuality' in Indian society acts as a factor responsible for creating 'capability deprivation' of women, impeding her ability to benefit from 'development'.

Obja Borah Hazarika in her study, "Women as Witches, Witches as Homo Sacer, Women as Homo Sacer?", presents an interesting theoretical exercise to understand the burning issue of witch hunting employing the concept of Homo Sacer provided by Giorgio Agamben. The study has attempted to examine how 'witch hunting' produces 'witches' as 'Homo Sacer' in today's society which in turn leads to a situation where they could be denied the basic human rights, legal rights or any other rights fundamental for a meaningful living. The author has also explored the societal, cultural, religious, and economic reasons which leads to the creation of the 'witch' as 'Homo Sacer' and has made a critical examination of the horrid phenomenon of witch hunting using a post-modernist framework provided by Agamben.

The study, "Reel and Real Indian Women", Sheetal J. Tamakuwala critically examines the popular Hindi films and television serials produced, the widespread influence on the Indian masses for last three to four decades and their capability for wish fulfilments and ignoring the reality. The author has designated these films and TV Serials as a micro world of escapism. The chapter argues that the mainstream films and TV serials (media) are now presenting women as a commercial item, a thing for pleasure and entertainment only. They further movies itself to a patriarchal coding which leaves little space for a feminist engagement. The author argues that the Films, TV serials and advertisements feeds myths and legends from time to the women which provides them with avenues for day-dreaming in the absence of a conscious identity with the complex social reality. The study further argues for getting rid of the dominant discourse by evolving an alternative discourse anchored in development and empowerment which will go a long way in the project of emancipation of women. Media should present women in different assertive roles instead of portraying them as housewives and sex symbols.

The study, "Gender Issues in Family Planning: A Case Study" by Maitreyee Sharma explores the current scenario of implicit and explicit gender issues that hinder the practice of family planning.

The study has been conducted among a scheduled tribe known as Mishing. Through an empirical investigation she has stressed upon the need of incorporating gender equity in the whole process of family planning for its effectiveness of fulfilment of the desired ends.

Upasana Borthakur in her study, "Status of Working Women: A Sociological Study Based in a Tea Estate of Assam" has taken up a simple yet significant issue that has its stronghold on Indian Society even today and which has negative impact when it comes to women and their status in our society in particular and gender equality in general. The study has focused on the fact that even today women work only out of economic necessity or to make an additional income for the household. Hence, they remain secondary earners in the family, perform dual responsibility of home and workplace and still get considered as secondary members of the society. In this light, the study has tried to evaluate the status of women workers from a tea estate in Dibrugarh district through an empirical enquiry into the social life, community life, health, education, working conditions, living conditions, household responsibilities etc. of these women and has attempted to determine their position at home and in the workplace both. The conclusions of this study suggest that although it seems that the economic independence generated by their work in the plantation provides them with equal status with men and considerable freedom, their overall position in society has remained low. The inequality between men and women extends almost to every sphere of life, in unequal job mobility, unequal occupational and social status. The study argues that patriarchy and capitalism are working simultaneously as sources of subordination for these women.

"Dalit Women: A Case of Three Tier Discrimination", the study by Dr. Parijat Pradhan highlights the threefold oppression that Dalit women faces in India, even today. They face caste oppression at the hands of the upper castes, as labourers they face class based oppression primarily at the hands of the upper and middle castes and finally as women they experience patriarchal oppression at the hands of all men, including men of their own caste. The study explores the intersection of multiple forms of discrimination and various forms and frequency of violence against these women.

The study "Powerlessness of Female Sexworkers in Relation to Condom Usage: A Socialist Feminist Analysis" by Sudeshna Mukherjee and Rashmi, C.K. attempts to understand the violation of health rights of Female Sex workers in Bangalore. Investigating various issues such as reasons for getting into sex work, *marital status,* condom use, condom negotiation and reasons for not using condoms among the sex workers the study focuses on the various internal and external factors that contribute towards manipulating the powers of female sex workers to negotiate safe sex and makes a feminist analysis of the same. The study finds that women's own beliefs, myths and misconception, their low level of confidence and capacity, lack of ability to bargain collectively, and their unquestioning acceptance of established power and social structures contribute to the exploitation, discrimination and domination of these sex workers and undermines their ability for condom negotiation and ensuring their own health.

The study entitled "Gender Disparity and Economic Empowerment of Women in relation with Flower Vending Business: A Primary Survey Analysis with Special Reference to Kolaghat Flower Market of Purba Medinipur District, West Bengal" authored by Labani Dey and S.A.H. Moinuddin seeks to analyse the gender disparity and economic empowerment of women flower vendors in Kolaghat flower market of Purba Medinipur district in Kolkata. The study finds that disparity exists in terms of economic status across gender which has three major components—income, savings and debt status. Male flower vendors are better off than the female in terms of these components. However, the study also reveals that despite this inequality, flower vending provides a significant way for these women to empower themselves, especially in regard to their economic decision making abilities.

The final chapter of the book "Trends in Feminist Thought: With Special Reference to Indian Feminism" by Rajni Bala presents a comprehensive description of the feminist movement and its ideology so far. The study focuses on the Third World feminism and throws light on Indian feminism as well.

We were very happy when the RC-10 (Gender and Society) of Indian Sociological Society decided to bring out another publication consecutively after the last publication, "Gender and Health: A Sociological Insight". We are humbled and truly honoured for the trust the committee put on us by giving us the responsibility of editing and bringing out this new book entitled, "Contemporary Indian Society: A Gendered Perspective". Hence, at the very beginning we thank all the members of the executive body of RC-10 (Gender and Sociology) of Indian Sociological Society. We must also take this opportunity to offer our sincere thanks to Professor Abha Chauhan for her constant support along with her words of encouragement while we were preparing this book. We are truly indebted to Professor Alak Kumar Buragohain, Honourable Vice Channcellor, Dibrugarh University, Assam and a renowned intellectual; for his trust and words of encouragement. We owe a great deal of gratitude towards Prof. Vinay Kumar Srivastava, Department of Anthropology, University of Delhi and Prof. B.N. Borthakur of Dibrugarh University, Assam for their kind help and valuable suggestions while preparing this book. We are also indebted to Chandan Sharma, Associate Professor, Department of History, Dibrugarh University for their constant help and support during preparation of this book despite their busy schedules. We must also offer our thanks here to Hriday Ranjan Kalita, Research Scholar, Department of Sociology, Dibrugarh University for his enthusiasm and efforts in preparing the manuscript of this edited book. My sincere thanks and gratitude also goes to all the contributors for their valuable works that this book has been comprised. Finally, we would also like to thank Concept Publishing Company Pvt. Ltd., for taking up the responsibility of publishing it. This book has an aim to highlight various issues and problems associated with women in India. While doing it, certain unintentional mistakes may have occurred. We hope that the intellectual society will embrace this work and will be kind enough to point out the errors so that we can modify them in the next edition of the book.

Jyoti Prasad Saikia
Shweta Prasad

List of Contributors

Dr. Abha Chauhan, Professor, Department of Sociology, University of Jammu, Jammu.

Dr. Arvinder A. Ansari, Associate Professor, Jamia Millia Islamia, New Delhi.

Dr. Dola Borkataki, Assistant Professor, Department of Sociology, K.K. Handiqui State Open University, Guwahati, Assam.

Hriday Ranjan Kalita, Research Scholar, Department of Sociology, Dibrugarh University, Dibrugarh, Assam.

Dr. Jyoti Prasad Saikia, Associate Professor, Department of Sociology, Dibrugarh University, Dibrugarh, Assam.

Labani Dey, Research Scholar, Department of Sociology, Vidyasagar University, West Bengal.

Dr. Maitreyee Sharma, Assistant Professor, Department of Anthropology, Dibrugarh University, Assam.

Dr. Obja Borah Hazarika, Assistant Professor, Department of Political Science, Dibrugarh University, Assam.

Dr. Parijat Pradhan, Assistant Professor in Centre for Sociological Studies, CUSB, Patna.

Dr. Rajni Bala, Head, Department of Sociology, B.U.C. College, Batala.

Rashmi, C.K., Research Scholar, Centre for Women's Studies, Bangalore University, Bangalore.

Dr. S.A.H. Moinuddin, Professor of Sociology, Department of Sociology, Vidyasagar University, West Bengal.

Dr. Sheetal J. Tamakuwala, Assistant Professor, MSW Programme, Department of Sociology, VNSG University, Surat, Gujarat.

Dr. Sudeshna Mukherjee, Assistant Professor, Centre for Women's Studies, Bangalore University, Bangalore.

Upasana Borthakur, Research Scholar, Department of Sociology, IGNOU, New Delhi.

1

Gender Studies and its Significance in Contemporary Society

Dola Borkataki

Gender studies is a young and emerging discipline. Despite its recent origin and short history it has undergone several transformations and a consensus regarding its concepts, methods and research subjects is still awaited. However, its inter-disciplinary nature and importance of the issues it deals with can be credited to have endowed it a special recognition in the academia. The growing interest in the research area on gender discourse is a clear testimony of its multi-disciplinary and interdisciplinary character, as the issues under its ambit can be understood and analysed from various disciplinary perspectives. The chapter makes an attempt to not only trace the emergence of Gender Studies as a discipline but also to comprehend its significance in the contemporary society.

'Gender' as an issue, has long been debated and deliberated upon. From the suffrage movement to the fight for equal opportunities in education and employment; from welfare to empowerment, emancipation, so on and so forth, gender based issues have been the focal point of Activism and subsequently the Academic discourse. The term or the concept of gender is a systematic way of understanding men and women socially and the patterning of relationships between them. In Sociological and Feminist thought, Gender indicates the cultural constitution comprising notions, perceptions, and premises concerning femininity and masculinity and the ways in which these serve ideologically to maintain gendered identities (Mishra, 2014).

Gender and Sex

Men and Women, from ages, have been seen as opposites in terms of their physical and mental setup; capacities and capabilities. They have been categorised as two different entities each capable of performing certain specific roles in society. Thus, traditionally the behaviour of man and woman has been assumed to be naturally different from one another with certain societal norms restricting their behaviour to their gendered identity. These differences in behaviour, roles and responsibilities between man and woman has become the core of analysis and the inquisitiveness to comprehend the basis of these differences as basically 'biological' or as 'social constructions' by the society have laid the foundations of study on gender. The construction of sex and gender; the perception of masculinity and femininity; the allocation of different roles and responsibilities based on these differences and gender stereotypes have laid the basis of 'Gender' as a serious issue for investigation, enquiry, and analysis. Gender studies have grown out of the need to address some of these issues in everyday life, as well as, on the global arena of international politics in which cultural, economic, political and social inequalities are played out.

The concept of gender in feminist writings and other sociological discourses became popular in the early 1970s. Academicians, Researchers and Feminist Scholars have used the term 'sex' and 'gender' to mark the difference between the biologically different male and female and between the socially different 'man' and 'woman'. Gender is conceptualised as a system that not only divides the human race into two categories but also privileges the male over the female. It operates as a set of hierarchically arranged roles in modern society which makes masculine half of the equation positive and the feminine negative (Francis *et al.*, 2003). In feminist analysis Gender is traditionally defined in relation to sex: gender as the cultural or social construction of sex. As a Sociological or Anthropological category, gender is not simply the gender one is, a man or a woman, but rather a set of meanings that sexes assume in particular societies (*ibid.*: 3).

Different thinkers, writers and scholars have provided different understandings and opinions on sex and gender. Judith Butler perceives sex as natural that came prior to gender. Gender is seen as a secondary construct which is imposed over the top of this natural distinction. Viewed thus, Butler argues 'sex' itself becomes a social category.

Ann Oakley in her book, 'Sex, Gender and Society' (1972) argued that the imposition of the roles of 'housewife' and 'mother' on women is because of their biology. The traditional roles assigned to men and women helps in maintaining the social fabric of the society and any effort to change their traditional roles can cause damage to this social fabric of the society. Oakley's key argument while deliberating upon the socially assigned roles of men and women was that this distribution or allotment of roles helps to support and maintain the patriarchal society. Simone de Beauvoir in her book 'The Second Sex' (1949) stated that "one is not born, but rather becomes a woman". She elucidates on how gender differences in society makes the man superior through his role as the bread winner. The economic importance of the role of man gives him a position of power in the society and family. Gender differences are set in hierarchal opposition such that men are superior and women are subordinate. Women's position is that of the 'other' and women are the continual outsiders.

Again Shulamith Firestone in her book, 'The Dialectics of Sex' (1970) sees patriarchy as exploiting women's biological capacity to reproduce as their essential weakness. According to her only by resorting to technological advances and freeing themselves from the burden of childbirth can women smash this oppression and get themselves rid of this oppressive patriarchal system. She advocated breaking down the biological bond between mothers and children by establishing communes where monogamy and nuclear family do not exist.

Thus sex and gender has been conceptualised, understood and explained in different ways. But to keep it simple, gender explains the differences between men and women in social terms as men, and what a man can do; and as woman and as what a woman can or cannot do. Therefore, gender is an analytical category that is socially constructed to differentiate the biological difference between men and women. The term gender is also used to describe the differences in behaviour between men and women which are described as 'masculine' and 'feminine'. Gender makes a difference not only because it sorts and categorizes humanity, but also because humanity is sorted and categorized by other discursive labels, such as class or race, by experiences in work, family and civic life, which interact with gender to produce a wide variety of outcomes (Essed *et al.*, 2005) Feminist writings focus on this aspect and claim that these differences are not biological but are social constructions of patriarchal society.

Gender Studies as a Discipline

The driving force behind gender studies is definitely feminism. Feminism is a both a political movement and a field of knowledge, the latter being called Feminist research or Feminist Theory. Feminism is the view that Women are oppressed in significant ways and this oppression should be ended. Even though feminist views have been expressed occasionally for hundreds of years, the first period of Feminist social activism in the United States began in the mid-nineteenth century with the Seneca Falls on Women's Rights Convention (Kramer, 2004). Across the world, the gender politics of second-wave feminism has been intertwined with the introduction of the concept of gender into the professional work of Sociologists (Rege, 2003). Sociologists and their professional bodies were being criticised by the Feminists for their andocentric character and patriarchal hegemony. It was accused as being Male-centric and Sex-blind in its content, methods and researches. They argued that Sociology despite its claim to be value neutral was a male stream discipline which had been mainly concerned with research on men and by implication with theories for men. Findings based on all male samples had been generalised for the whole population, and issues and areas that concerned women were seen as personal and outside the purview of the academic (*Ibid.*: 4). Since, then there were several efforts made to focus on the issues and experiences of women. Women's experiences came to seen as significantly different from men and Women's perspectives were incorporated as theories and subjects of study. However, again the feminist theorization with 'woman' as the central category of analysis has been criticised and challenged in the last two decades as being a homogenized notion. Post Modern Feminism have challenged the idea of Women as a homogenized category and argued that feminist goals could not be conceptualized in terms of the needs and interests of white, middle-class women (*Ibid.*: 6). They have argued in favour of intersectional analysis of the issues and experiences of women, as women do not constitute a homogenous category. Thus there occurred a shift from woman to gender because gender as a conceptual category allows the analysis of interlocking structure of oppression, namely race, gender, class etc. As the point of focus shifted from women to gender even the courses and curriculums had to be renamed as Sociology of Gender. The study and researches on sex roles led to the initiation of the study of gender in Sociology. Contemporary Sociologists views social life itself as gendered: experiences, opportunities, and burdens are differently available to males and females because of social views about maleness and femaleness (Kramer, 2004).

However, the use of the term 'Gender' has also been subject to several challenges and contestations. Some scholars prefer the term 'Women' over 'Gender' because for them the use of the category 'Gender' shifts the focus on the specific issues of women in academics as well as political arena. But those for whom 'Gender' is the apt category for analysis argues that Gender as a conceptual category allows for a more inclusive analysis of human experience based on intersecting structures of domination, difference and diversity (Rege, 2003). The Third World, Black and *Dalit* Feminists have opposed the use of 'Women' as homogenous, over-arching category. They have highlighted the potential dangers of assuming the category of women as homogeneous and identical. They have argued that while the category of women universalizes and homogenizes the experiences of white, middle-class and upper-caste women, the use of the category of Gender on the other hand allows for the analysis of differences of race, class, caste, nation and sexual orientation between women. Gender as a category allows for an analysis of the interlocking structures of oppression and, in fact, goes beyond the analysis of the differences among women by underlining the gendered nature of caste and class oppression (*Ibid*.: 9, 10). Thus they advocate the use 'Gender' as a category because of its 'all inclusive' characteristic.

Gender studies, therefore, is an area of interdisciplinary study committed to the understanding and analysis of gender identity and gendered representations in its different facets. It includes studies of women, men, queer so on and so forth. Being inter-disciplinary in nature it draws on knowledge from humanities, social sciences, medicine etc. Gender Research is mostly focused on the correlation or relationship between knowledge, power and gender and how it intersects with other social categories such as ethnicity, class, sexuality, nationality, age, disability. Gender Studies can be understood as an attempt to comprehend power relations. It makes an effort to understand the power relations and politics in every aspect of society is it social, economic or cultural and every social relationship. It scrutinizes the structures of oppression and the processes through which economic, social and cultural forces intersect in different contexts. The "power" is understood as being born from 'patriarchy'. Gender divide has been reinforced by the patriarchal system and this system or regime excludes women from the positions of power and authority. Gender Studies enable us to understand and analyse this system that privileges the man over the woman and also how the experiences of women belonging to different categories of are different. Gender studies and researches have been inspired and influenced by various scholarly traditions, such as empiricism, Marxism, psychoanalysis, post-structuralism, critical race theory, inter-sectionality and post-colonial theory, queer studies, lesbian, gay, bi and trans studies (so-called LGBT studies), critical studies of sexualities, body theory, sexual difference feminisms, black feminisms, ecological feminisms so on and so forth. The field of study has, in an accelerating pace, grown and expanded across the globe, and has contributed to the emergence of a diversity of specific national and regional developments.

Gender Studies enable critical analysis of gender and its inter-linkages with various social institutions (caste, class, state); and how these institutions mediate and position men and women in different ways. It emphasises on the holistic and structural understanding and analysis of class, race, and gender how they are intertwine in giving rise to a hegemonic structure. LGBT, Women, Men studies, and other sources of oppression and violence of state against the people are all subjects of investigation and study in Gender Studies and hence, it provides a holistic understanding of the everyday life experiences of people and how the social system privileges some over the other. Thus, Gender Studies has an advantage of proving a nuanced understanding of social relations.

Though gender studies may not come across as a strictly professional course—besides research work and teaching—there are opportunities for gender experts in international institutions from World Bank to the UN, women's institutions, companies and NGOs.

REFERENCES

Anne, Francis Cranny, Wendy Waring, Pam Stavrpoulos, Joan Kirkby (2003). *Gender Studies—Terms and Debates*, Palgrave Macmillan, New York.

Kramer, Laura (2004). *The Sociology of Gender—A Brief Introduction*, Rawat Publications, New Delhi.

Rege, Sharmila (2003). *Sociology of Gender*, Sage Publications, New Delhi.

Woodward, Kath and Sophie Woodward: *Gender studies and interdisciplinarity*, Palgrave Communications. 1:15018 doi: 10.1057/palcomms.2015.18

WEBSITES

https://www.tema.liu.se/tema-g/grundutb/a-brief-history-of-gender-studies?l=en

http://www.thehindu.com/features/education/why-gender-studies/article5716899.ece

http://www.archive.mu.ac.in

https://whydoesitmattercanada.wordpress.com/2013/07/16/why-do-gender-studies-matter/

2

Minority Within Minority

Understanding Muslim Women's Activism in India

Arvinder A. Ansari

Women have always been negotiating the personal with the political or we can say there seems an unending tussle between their private self and the public (community) domain. The case is not different for India's Muslim women who continue to battle for their identity though without any breakthrough so far in an environment where Islamic feminist activism still is not an organized 'social movement'.

The notion that 'Muslim women' is minority within minority represents a distinct category and has thus gained a symbolic importance as part of the wider discourse of 'communalism' in India. 'Communalism' refers to the notion that Muslims and Hindus constitute separate and antagonistic groups. Within this discourse 'Muslim women' stand as symbol of the Muslim community as a whole, both for Muslim conservative groups as well as for members of the Hindu Right, who echo orientalist discourse by arguing that it is the oppression of Muslim women by Muslim men that proves the inferiority and backwardness of Muslims in general (*see* Bacchetta, 1994).

Studies of Muslim women in India view Muslim women as a subgroup within the wider 'Indian Muslim community'. Such construction is also influenced by a more general interest in studying Muslim women across the world. The intellectual curiosity in Muslim women has its underpinnings in the orientalist enchantment with the veil and the harem, which has painted a picture of Muslim women as symbols of the insensitivity of colonised people and the symbolic 'Other' to Europe's rational civilisation (*see* Mabro, 1991; Lazreg, 1998; Yegenoglu, 2003). In the Indian context in particular, contemporary concern with studying and understanding Muslim women increased greatly during the 1970s when the cause of 'Third World women', more particularly 'Muslim women' often assumed to be the most oppressed members of this group—became the focus of attention for Western feminists (*see* Mohanty, 1988). Lot of scholarly interest was generated to study 'Indian Muslim women' during the mid-1980s and early 1990s in response to the national debates occurring around the issue of personal laws during the Shah Bano controversy in 1986, (Discussed Below). A series of studies have been published since this time that look at the social problems of Muslim women, beginning with the premise that Muslim women are disadvantaged in particular ways because of their religious identity and gender hence focusing on issues related to personal laws, veil and segregation (*see* Lateef, 1990; Kazi, 1999; Hasan and Menon, 2006).

The focus of this chapter is to understand: Are Muslim women in India empowered to deny patriarchy, and ignore customary laws? Or if they are able to cross over the hurdles of the patriarchal society; what are the ways or mechanisms through which one can see Muslim women climbing up the ladder of equality doctrine today? This chapter is trying to argue and understand the contradictory pulls of culture, religion, law and politics that play upon her life and how does she position herself within these contradictory thresholds of customary laws and feminism? This chapter explores the complexities, negotiations and contradictions entailed in the process of claiming a "Muslim" identity in an attempt to complicate the present understandings of this activism. The larger question for discussion is how activism of the Muslim Women's networks have negotiated theses spaces. More importantly, how does she relate to the vocal, visible and highly articulate women's movement that brought gender concerns within the political arena. In the first section an attempt has been made to locate Muslim women in wider women's movement, disenchantment of minority women from secular women's movement and emergence of Muslim Women activism in the aftermath of Shah Bano judgement and subsequent communalisation of Indian society. The second section of the chapter is analysing the engagement of prominent Muslim women organisations and networks, their vision and mission to fight for Muslim Women rights and promote gender justice and equality within the community.

Minority within Minority: Locating Muslim Women in Feminist Movement in India

Muslim women in India face considerable challenges as citizens and as members of the largest minority. They suffer from many disadvantages in areas such as education, employment and access to welfare programmes. As pointed by Hasan and Menon (2006) the status of Muslim women broadly indicates the shortage of three essentials: knowledge (measured by literacy and average years of schooling), economic power (captured through participation in paid work and income), and autonomy (measured by decision making and physical mobility) as the defining features of women's low status. Further the contestation between personal laws and constitutional law has subjugated her rights and this is viewed as major stumbling block in her empowerment.

Since its inception, the contemporary women's movement has had an indifferent relationship with religion. Sands (2008) mentions that the Indian women's movement was influenced by the growth of second-wave feminism around the world at the time, which for the most part rejected religion as being inherently patriarchal and was committed to the political project of secularism. Despite this ambivalent relationship with religion, some sections of the movement have also attempted to positively engage with religious discourses and symbols, but have focused almost exclusively on Hindu religious imagery. Sunder Rajan (1998: WS36) points to the strategic co-optation of religious symbolism by some members of the women's movement who 'invoked "traditional" (read: Hindu) symbols in some cases as a means of diluting, if not countering, the Western bias of "feminism"'. The use of goddess imagery, such as the naming of the first feminist publishing house, 'Kali for Women', and celebrations of women's spirituality, spearheaded by Madhu Kishwar in the journal *Manushi*, can be seen as attempts to broaden the women's movement's appeal by 'indigenising' feminism (Kirmani, 2011: 3). Same has been affirmed by Omvedt (1993: 205-

06) in context of eco-feminist movement, it has also been receptive to religious language and symbolism with the idea of *Prakriti* (nature) or the feminine nurturing force within Hinduism, being celebrated as a reclamation of 'tradition' for women. These developments, although limited in extent and debated among their supporters, may have inadvertently contributed to the alienation of non-Hindu women from the women's movement (Agnes, 1995; Sunder Rajan, 1998).

The Shah Bano controversy marked a decisive moment in the history of women's movement in India. Shah Bano, an elderly Muslim woman from Madhya Pradesh, had filed a case for maintenance from her ex-husband after almost fifty years of marriage in 1978 and was granted a small amount of maintenance by the Indore Magistrate's Court, which was later, increased marginally by the Madhya Pradesh High Court. This decision was disputed by her husband as a violation of Muslim personal law and was taken to the Supreme Court in 1985. The Supreme Court ruled in favour of Shah Bano, arguing that she was entitled to maintenance, which upheld the right of a divorced Muslim woman for maintenance under the Criminal Procedure Code Section 125. Furthermore, the Supreme Court judgement called for the abolition of separate personal laws and the creation of a Uniform Civil Code (UCC). The Supreme Court's judgement prompted strong protests by bodies such as the All India Muslim Personal Law Board (AIMPLB), which was established in 1973 with the express purpose of protecting Muslim personal law from state intervention. The AIMPLB and its supporters mobilised around the idea that 'Islam was in danger', arguing that a secular court could not decide on matters related to *sharia* and especially on matters related to the home and family (Agnes, 2004). In order to counter the Supreme Court's verdict, a Member of Parliament, G.M. Banatwala, drafted a Bill that sought to exclude Muslim women from the purview of the Criminal Procedure Code and thousands were rallied in its support around the country by the AIMPLB (Kumar, 1994: 84). The government introduced a Bill in the Parliament, yielding to the pressure exerted by the Muslim orthodoxy, excluding divorced Muslim women from the purview of Section 125 of Cr.P.C. This move was considered most blatant instance of the defeat of the principle of gender justice for by the secular women's movement in India. They felt that Act not only deprived divorced Muslim women of the rights granted under a secular provision, Sec. 125 Cr.P.C. on the basis of religion alone but also violated the Constitutional mandate of equality (Agnes, 2002). The fallout of this was the large scale campaign organized by the women's movement, to evade the question of religious identity by focusing on Shah Bano's right to equality and dignity as a citizen of India and not as a member of a particular religious community which was in line with the movement's overall secular approach till then. *Shah Bano case* became political bait in the hands of the Hindu Right. They used this case as a political opportunity. Hindu nationalist groups argued in support of Uniform Civil Code (UCC), citing the opposition to the *Shah Bano case* as evidence of Muslim 'backwardness' and resistance to national integration. Muslim women and personal law became a terrain on which political battles were fought between Hindu Right and Muslim conservative groups. Hindu Right argued that the Muslim Women's Bill was an example of the 'minority appeasement' and 'pseudo-secularism' practiced by the ruling party, forgetting the resentment of Hindu revivalists during the 1950s debates over the Hindu Code Bill, which legislated on Hindu personal laws (Hasan, 1994, 1998; Kishwar, 1998; Kumar, 1994).

Women's groups protested the government's pandering to religious conservatives as vote bank politics at the expense of women's rights (Butalia, 2002: 17). Passing of the Muslim Women's (Protection of Rights on Divorce) Act (1986) raised serious questions of representation for the women's movement in terms of the caste, class and religious backgrounds of its members, as well as calling into question its supposedly secular stance in the face of wider processes of religious consolidation and polarisation taking place in India at the time.

The debate on Muslim personal laws alongside the selective use of Hindu religious imagery led some critics of the women's movement (Agnes, 1995, 2002) and (Sunder Rajan, 2003) to argue that the women's movement had not developed a clearly secular position. The women's movement's orientation of a liberal-democratic approach to secularism advocating separation between religion and politics left little choice but to campaign for a Uniform Civil Code, rather than explore alternative avenues for reconciling religious identity and gender-related concerns (*see* Kumar, 1994; Menon, 2011). The passage of the Muslim Women's Protection Act

(1986) was seen as a defeat by the women's movement, the ripple effects of the activism surrounding the *Shah Bano case* continued long after in the 1990s, creating cracks among the members of women's movement which had further escalated with Hindu women's participation in the massive violence in the destruction of the mosque, and against the Muslim community in 1992 in the aftermath of the demolition and it was again repeated in 2002 in Gujarat Violence, this questioned the category of "woman" itself. The women's movement could no longer envision an unmarked "woman" available for mobilization, forcing members of the women's movement to critically reflect on questions related to communalism, secularism and representation (*see* Butalia, 2002).

The feminist movement, too, had to confront the reality that it was, itself, marked by a majoritarian identity and symbols, whereby "Muslim" appeared as something different and aberrant from its discourse. In an attempt to circumvent criticisms of being alien to local culture and Western in orientation, the women's movement, despite being secular, had adopted symbols of female power from Hindu mythology. Very few women from minority communities were present in these organizations; those that were, were in turn trying to prove their secular credentials by trying to fit in (Agnes, 1995: 137-143; Subramaniam 2006: 50). This uncomfortable position *vis-à-vis* religion and Muslim women's rights in particular would continue to haunt the women's movement, with no reforms made to date on Muslim personal laws. Marginalization of Muslim Women's rights in post Shah Bano controversy and subsequent victimization of Muslim women's in communal riots of 1993, 2002, and 2013 highlighted the sense of alienation among minority women and those from marginalized communities.

Anti-Women *Fatwas*: Muffled Voices

As the discussion above demonstrates, the manner in which the *Shah Bano case* unfolded and the subsequent events of communal violence and marginalization meant that Muslim women were under pressure to subordinate their gender concerns (Hussain, 2007: 72-73). As community boundaries have hardened, Muslim women have borne the brunt of identity politics in terms of violence (from outside the community) and control over their life choices (from within the community). Flavia Agnes sums up the double marginalization of Muslim women thus: the intersectionality of Muslim women cannot be accommodated in a "raceless tale of gender subordination," nor in a "gender-less narrative of minority victimization for the Muslim community" (Agnes, 2002: 3698).

Discussions on Muslim women continued to focus on their status within the community and position in Muslim Personal Law even though they are also the most likely to belong to low-income, low-educational-attainment, low-aspiration groups, along with being among the most vulnerable citizens of society (Hasan and Menon, 2006: 2-7). *Shah Bano case* brought the 'plight of the Indian Muslim woman' onto the national stage. Her case highlighted the dilemmas of contending identity-based declarations in a political environment that was becoming increasingly polarised along religious lines. Muslim women oppression was once again brought to national attention with the case of Gudiya in 2004 and then of Imrana in 2005. The conservative *Ulema* (Muslim religious scholars) yet again took it upon itself to represent 'the Muslim community'. Throughout these debates the voices of Muslim women speaking for themselves were rarely heard in public debates. *Gudiya's case* is the most tragic of them all. Her husband Arif, who was serving in the Indian army in Kashmir, became a prisoner of war and was unheard of for five years. Subsequently, she married Taufiq and when she was pregnant from this second marriage, the first husband returned and expressed his desire to reunite with his wife. When reported in the media, television channels hopped into the tussle and publicly paraded the anguish of a young girl, one channel went to the extent of holding a live 'panchayat', which projected the eight months pregnant girl burning with fever. The panchayat gave its verdict in full public view that Gudiya should now return to her first husband and it is his prerogative either to accept her first child or discard it. All the channels had a field day projecting this story and interviews with various relatives of the three persons concerned and Muslim *maulavis*. Finally, it seemed that Arif had agreed to accept the child and Gudiya was happy to keep the child. Though in her earlier interviews she had made a caustic comment: ***"Yeh koi khel thody hai, aaj iske saath kal uske saath*** (This is no game. Living with someone today, another tomorrow)". (*see* Agnes, Shah bano to Kauser Bano). But after the verdict, she returned to her husband's home as reported in *Indian*

Express, she was calm, composed and relaxed and commented that this is her destiny and further endorsed this statement with a comment that it is her wish. Unfortunately a few months later Gudiya passed away and her voice was stifled with her burial, without any public debate on how Gudiya died.

In another case, Imrana was allegedly raped by her father-in-law. Upon her complaint, another quasi-judicial court with the help of a local *Maulvi* declared her *haram*, or forbidden to her husband, and she was told to leave her marital home, while the father-in-law went scot-free. It was only with the intervention by women's groups that the father-in-law was booked and his subsequent bail applications thwarted. Both cases caught national attention and received enormous media publicity followed by a blitz of anti-Muslim coverage. Although such quasi-judicial systems operate across all communities, in the case of the Muslim community it is difficult to appeal against the rulings. As Muslim Personal Law remains uncodified, there is no legal protection for the Muslim woman. The combination of self-reflection within the movement together with the burgeoning of various types of NGOs as well as the general diversification of the political sphere has led to the emergence of new forms of identity-based organizing both within and apart from the women's movement by women of marginalized communities who address multiple axes of power based on gender, caste, religion and class (Zaman, 2013).

Active Voices of Muslim Women Organisations: A Glimpse

Women's activism has started very late in India. The inherent patriarchal structure of Indian society was not very accommodative with women raising voices for their rights. Nonetheless, it started during the era of late 70s with a very Hindu feminist undertone, which needs to be studied separately. However, since the 1990s, several individuals and groups of Muslim women activists have emerged across India and are working to change this situation by claiming their right to represent themselves. Vatuk's (2008) pioneering ethnographic study of Muslim women's organizations in India mentions the emergence of these groups founded in order to pursue the goal of legal reforms, nor to create more publicity for the Islamic feminist agenda.

Most of these organizations have emerged from local grass-roots initiatives, first among these is Mumbai Based oldest Muslim women organisation Awaaz-e-Niswan (AeN), it had taken important initiatives, which have gone beyond personal laws to promote gender equality. They aim to provide aid and support to poor, illiterate and marginalised women, while at the same time raising their consciousness about the gender inequities that exist in society and the need to strive to overcome them. Their engagement with legal reform is an outgrowth of these broad-based activities. Much like other women's groups Muslim women's groups engage with a range of issues that include education, employment and domestic violence. These services are not only available to Muslim women exclusively. Nor does the way in which this counselling is carried out refer to a specific Muslim tradition, but rather follows a pattern which according to Vatuk (2008) is very typical for the world of feminist or women's NGOs in India. Although these efforts have not to date inspired the development of a major reform movement among Muslims, they represent vital steps in seeking to build a rights-based movement.

The other organization, named the Muslim Women's Rights Network (MWRN), was founded in 1999 by activists from AeN and from the Mumbai-based Women's Research and Action Group (WRAG), is the most successful network with a nationwide radius. WRAG conducted an extensive study in 1994-98, titled "Women and Law in the Muslim Community", with the declared aim of collecting, documenting and analysing the diverse civil or family laws that are applied to Muslims in India. It is often over-looked that the term Muslim Personal Law (MPL) does not refer to a codified or unified family law code and that laws may differ more or less significantly from region to region (Mahmood, 1986, 1993). One of the findings of this research project was that Muslim women in India clearly support the demand for reform of Muslim Personal Law in India (Nainar, 2000). As WRAG/MWRN describes on its homepage, it was this claim, which among other things, led to an increase in awareness-rising campaigns, which shall help to inform Muslim women about the rights that are guaranteed to them in the Quran (holy book of Muslims) and thereby encourage new impulses for debate on reform of MPL. The present very active group named Bharatiya Muslim Mahila Andolan (BMMA) was formed more recently in 2005. Although the BMMA advocacy deals with the issue of matrimonial rights and the reform of Muslim Personal Laws, it also tackles broader issues facing the community including socio-economic and political deprivation. BMMA claims to be the first pan-Indian movement uniting Muslim women across the various existing castes and classes in Muslim Indian society. It is this organization that most explicitly states its reference to the global discourse of Islamic feminism in the formulation of goals by declaring that BMMA strives "to explore possibilities of reforming personal laws based on male dominance"(Schneider, 2009: 66). Both networks—Muslim Women's Rights Network (MWRN) and the Bharatiya Muslim Mahila Andolan (BMMA)—are challenging the notion that Muslim women are voiceless victims by asserting their political agency. In so doing, they question the authority of conservative Muslim male-dominated forums such as the All India Muslim Personal Law Board (AIMPLB) to speak for the Muslim community, as well as changing the face of the women's movement, which has had a troubled relationship with religion in the past. The emerging Muslim women-led networks in India are challenging the authority of the religious elite to represent the 'Muslim community' while re-framing the category 'Muslim women' in order to assert political agency.

Both networks move beyond looking at Muslim women's issues as consisting only of *pardah* (veiling and segregation), polygamy and triple *talaq* (divorce), which have been the main tropes through which 'Muslim women' have been constructed and understood as a category in the Indian context. The BMMA does this by placing the exclusion of Muslim women in the wider context of the exclusion faced by Muslims in India in general. Similarly, the MWRN expands the scope of the issues associated with Muslim women by drawing attention to problems related to violence against the community as a whole, and women in particular, as well as addressing issues related to the targeting of Muslims by the state apparatus. This does not mean that the issue of personal laws is forgotten, but rather, that both networks are attempting to contextualize the multiple disadvantages and insecurities faced by Muslim women in a broader pattern of economic, social political exclusion of Muslim community as pointed in Sachar Committee Report (Sachar, 2006: 19-20).

In contrast to the MWRN, which does not explicitly use religion as a campaigning tool and is committed to a secular approach, the BMMA is experimenting with Islamic feminist approaches, asserting that it is not Islam *per se* that has oppressed Muslim women, but centuries of male interpretation of Islamic texts. Members of the BMMA argue that standing up for women's rights does not have to mean abandoning one's religious identity, and are involved in projects that encourage women to engage with Islamic texts in order to be able to claim their rights, including those related to inheritance, marriage, and political empowerment. Such efforts are pioneering steps in the Indian context where little attempt has previously been made to reconcile religion and feminism. In a context in which Muslims feel increasingly under attack, such a reformist approach may prove to be an effective strategy. However, as many members of the MWRN point out, it may also limit the terms of the debate to the confines of religious discourse, leaving little or no space to those who are not believers themselves or who feel that religion should remain a private matter. This approach may also have limited appeal in a context where many within the Muslim community feel that their religious identities are being threatened and are hence less receptive to reformist ideas.

The MWRN and the BMMA also represent important developments in the context of the women's movement in India and can be seen as a sign of the movement's fragmentation and diversification. While the MWRN feels that it is an important part of the movement, the BMMA sees itself as separate from the mainstream women's movement. Hasina Khan, who is a leader within the MWRN and works with the Mumbai-based group Awaaz-e-Niswan, feels that it is important to work within the wider women's movement: "Muslim women do need to make a space for themselves, but this does not mean that Muslim women make their own space and also carry out their struggle alone. If we say this, then we might become divided.... then we will not be able to call ourselves a women's movement. There will be a Muslim women's movement, a Hindu women's movement, a Christian women's movement" (as cited in Kirmani, 2009: 35).

Members of the MWRN argue that the women's movement has created space for Muslim women. However, they also admit that there is a need for more support from within the movement, and they are actively working to engage with women across communal boundaries in order to fight against the ghettoization of Muslim women's issues. On the other hand, members of the BMMA are critical of the women's movement's historical upper caste bias as well as its aversion to religion. BMMA members argue that the leaders of the women's movement have not gone far enough in cultivating new leadership, especially amongst women from marginalized communities. It is for this reason that members of the BMMA feel that it is crucial for Muslim women to build their own movement.

The activists who came together to form the BMMA felt that an organization for Muslim women should be one that attaches a positive value to "Muslim" and "Islam". This notion represents a significant difference from the approach of the MWRN and the BMMA acknowledges the role and importance of religion and culture in women's lives and seeks to positively reclaim those structures (Schneider, 2009). Although there is a broad spectrum of engagement with Islam (as a faith) within the BMMA, there is strong sense of identification with "Muslim" as a socio-cultural identity. This position stresses the value that culture holds for this minority community, including its women challenging the view that culture and religion, especially Islam, are only oppressive. On the other hand, members of the BMMA are more forthright in arguing that the women's movement and civil society in general have failed to address the needs of women from marginalised communities and to engage positively with religion. Zakia Jowher, founder member of BMMA, describes the position *vis-à-vis* the women's movement:

> "In our vision mission document it is very clear that we will always build our struggle along with other excluded people, which includes all of the *dalits* and *adivasis*, all other women, and the workers, labourers, all other excluded people.... We are very clear that whosever's fight it is, they are the ones who should lead. We don't need a *brahmin* woman to come and lead us... If for 60 years we haven't received justice, it is because the males have led, and within the women's it is always women from creamy layer"(Kirmani 2009: 20).

While these groups may differ in their strategies for women's rights advocacy, they are in agreement about the need to challenge the prerogative of male-dominated institutions such as the

AIMPLB to speak for the Muslim community. Many Muslim women activists joined the board called All India Muslim Women's Personal Law Board (AIMWPLB) and its decision-making bodies to draw attention to and resolve women's issues under the Muslim personal law. For example, to put an end to the predicament of triple *talaq,* some female members prepared a model marriage contract (*nikahnama),* which allowed women to stipulate conditions in the contract such as an option for delegated divorce (*talaq-e-tawfiz*), through which the husband permits his wife to initiate divorce at her own will, and presented it to the board for approval. However, the male-dominated board rejected it on the claim that it was an "un-Islamic" proposal and swiftly silenced uncompliant women's voices throughout the organization.

The AIMWPLB released a new *nikahnama* in 2008 that consisted of seventeen-point guidelines for marriage for bride and groom under the Islamic Law (*hidayatnama*) and an eight-point section on divorce process. Ms. Shaista Amber, President of the AIMWPLB, reports that it prohibits triple *talaq* through text messaging, email, video-conferencing, or phone, and recognizes women's right to delegated divorce (*Talaq-e-tawfiz*) and *Khul*. The model *nikahnama* also details women's right to post-marital maintenance and *Mehr*. To pre-empt the possible attacks of the traditional *Ulema* on the new *nikahnama,* the new marriage contract carries extensive quotes from relevant verses of the Quran.

In addition, AIMWPLB has established its own court structure (*mahila adalat*), deciding cases according to a women-friendly interpretation of *Sharia*. The women's court is located in Lucknow and convenes every Friday at a local mosque. Ms. Shaista Amber had reported that fifty couples have married under the new *nikahnama,* as it steadily gains acceptance in the community (as citied in Sezgin). It also deals with divorce cases, both male and female judges (*qazis*) sit together at *mahila adalat*. The law applied is not substantively different from the Sharia law applied by AIMPLB courts, but *qazis* at the *mahila adalat* implement it with an eye to "universal standards of human and women's rights"(*See* Sezgin). The BMMA working to secure the rights of women through feminist and humanist interpretations of Islam, has taken the women's cause one step further and made history by allowing a female *qazi,* Syeda Hamid, to solemnize a *nikah* (marriage) ceremony where all four witnesses were also women. (as quoted in Sezgin, 2012). While the members of the mainstream *ulema* questioned whether a woman could solemnize marriage under the Islamic law, BMMA silently broke the tradition and opened a new page for Muslim women in India who could rely on neither the secular state nor male-dominated communal institutions but their own initiative to end the discrimination they suffer under Muslim Personal Laws.

The activism of these networks illustrates important initiatives, which have gone beyond personal laws to promote gender equality. They aim to provide aid and support to poor, illiterate and marginalised women, while at the same time raising their consciousness about the gender inequities that exist in society and the need to strive to overcome them. Their engagement with legal reform is an outgrowth of these broad-based activities. Much like other women's groups Muslim women's groups engage with a range of issues that include education, employment and domestic violence (Hasan, 2010). Although these efforts have not to date inspired the development of a major reform movement among Muslims, they represent vital steps in seeking to build a rights-based movement. There are, for the first time, the beginnings of serious debate on social reform. But before getting into the discussion about the reforms, one needs to understand the challenges faced by these organisations and networks to take on to activism.

Although no further legal reforms have taken place with regard to Muslim women's rights since the Shah Bano affair, the presence of Muslim women-led networks alone marks a significant shift in the Indian political landscape. The appearance of the MWRN and the BMMA demonstrates the diversification of the women's movement, and of the political sphere in general as women from marginalized communities find new ways to engage with and challenge structures of power and authority at multiple levels. Their efforts are creating a space for Muslim women to actively engage in redefining their identities and reformulating relations of power within an increasingly constrained and polarised political context, one in which feminists have little room to manoeuvre outside of the confines of religious boundaries.

Muslim Women's Feminism: Challenges and Dilemmas

Muslim women activism has come often under attack from their own community. Most of the time they have to defend themselves against both direct attacks and subtler, deceptive whispers from the religious leadership and from members of the wider community, including male members of their own families. The activities they engage in often prevent their conforming strictly to orthodox standards of seclusion and Islamic femininity. They are also susceptible to criticism for being engaged in activities where they jeopardize the community honour in being inadvertently tricked into participating in dubious activities harmful to the community, thus accusing them for putting their interests as women ahead of the community's need to maintain a united front against the communal forces rampant in the society at large. (*see* Vatuk, 2008; Schneider, 2009; Zaman, 2013).

Though large number of Indian young women are being educated in women's *madrasas*, some even earning the title of *alima* ('female scholar'), but very few of them have shown proclivity to involve themselves publicly in fighting for women's rights, even those who succeed in presenting themselves as devout Muslims can be dismissed as lacking in scholarly qualifications, whenever they begin to cite the Quran or other religious sources to support their demands for gender justice. Their Islamic credentials are consistently questioned. Although growing numbers of activists argue that one doesn't need to be a highly-trained religious expert in order to read the Quran and discover for oneself that Indian Muslim women today are not being given their God-given rights (Vatuk, 2008: 512).

In case women activist are associated with non-sectarian women's organisations or to Muslim organisations that work closely with secular ones on controversial issues of current concern to Muslims than the intensity of their loyalty to the community is often questioned as well they may be suspected either of knowingly allowing themselves to be used by politicians. Most of these discussions have grown out of the debates surrounding Muslim personal laws and have, therefore, focused to a large degree on the issue of women's matrimonial rights. Schneider (2009) argues that there exists a dilemma within the women activists, despite sharing with self-identified feminists 'a theoretical perspective and a practice that criticizes social and gender inequalities, aims at women's empowerment, and seeks to transform knowledge, there is reluctance to claim that they are a 'feminist' since the term has quite negative connotations, not only within Muslim community but in India more generally. While campaigning for women's rights before a Muslim audience, they wish to avoid the term as it calls up images of an markedly Westernized woman, unfeminine, aggressive, antagonistic towards men, and careless of domestic and family responsibilities. Thus, they shy away from adopting the label for themselves (*see* Zaman, 2013 and Vatuk, 2008). Ms. Uzma Naheed, an Islamic Scholar is of the opinion that it is important to be in the good books of clergy and speak the language of *Sharia,* she said that she was able to sustain her struggle for women's rights as she has good terms with the AIMPLB leadership because, they know "I am working for women,. It is because our religion has given us rights that I am doing, they know that I am not a feminist" (Vatuk, 2008: 513).

There exists difference of opinion about whether and how to work with the *ulema* on issues of Personal Law. Some activists felt that being not strongly feminist helps. Most Muslim-led women's NGOs do maintain contacts witn local *qazis* or the *imams* of nearby mosques and regularly seek the cooperation. Some spend considerable time and effort trying to develop relationships with and keep open lines of communication with the local religious authorities. But they are often frustrated by these men's frequent reluctance or refusal to heed their recommendations when dealing with issues that affect women's well being.

In spite of this reluctance, all the Muslim women's networks have tried into dialogue with the higher religious leadership, in particular with the AIMPLB. Those who are themselves members of this Board naturally believe in working closely with the *ulema,* exerting whatever influence they can from within, they believed in positive approach rather than confrontational'. Some women activists had shared with Vatuk (2008) that since masses have great respect for the *ulema,* it is counter-productive to tell women not to heed what they say. It is much better to show that one is willing to give them proper deference and work with them to the extent possible. The MWRN and some of the smaller coalitions, positioned well outside the AIMPLB and not so averse to confrontation, have on different occasions invited members of the Board and other prominent clerics to discuss issues of women and the law. Though, there is still a large gap between what most women activists would like to see the AIMPLB do and the steps that it has actually taken, there are clear signs that the reformist women's voices are being heard by the members of this body and are even having some impact—though hardly a dramatic one—on their decision-making. Some women are pleased by the results of their efforts to exchange ideas with the Board, while others are discouraged by what they perceive as an absence of positive results. In order to overcome the impasse, both networks employ a kind of 'strategic essentialism' (Spivak, 1989, 1990, 1993) and use the unifying category of Muslim women as a means of exerting rights. This tactical use of Muslim women wrests the category out of the hands of the Hindu Right and the male-dominated *ulema* in order to assert a feminist political stance that recognises the importance of religious identity without sacrificing women's rights. Muslim women who are pressing for social and legal change in pursuit of gender equity always have to concern themselves about 'framing' the issue of women's rights in such a way that they are not 'put on the defensive and made to prove that they are not spouting alien and Western concepts', forced, as these women are to operate within a context wherein a more radical secular feminist approach is certain to attract strong community antagonism, an Islamic feminist approach may indeed be the wisest choice.

Codification of Islamic Laws

The project of legal reform is greatly complicated by the problems confronting the Muslim community, which remains a vulnerable minority in India. A high-level committee on the status of the Muslim community, known as the Sachar Committee, has shown that they are impoverished, marginalised and under-represented in public institutions. They do, however, have the right to have their own personal laws and to continue to practise these under state protection (*See* Sachar Report 2006). From the point of view of Muslim women this has meant that the articulation of gender interests has been tightly controlled and articulated within the terms of an identity discourse.

Both Muslims and Muslim women continue to be defined by birth-bound identities, and consequently the notion that Muslim women's status is attributable to certain intrinsic, immutable, 'Islamic' features is widely prevalent. All the debates tend to revolve around either the desirability of reform from within the community and with religious sanction in order to preserve a Muslim identity, or on the need to transcend community and end the gender discrimination inherent in personal laws by working towards a uniform civil code that will govern all citizens. Political negotiations over personal laws have invariably favoured conservative voices among Muslims to the detriment of women's voices and women's rights. In order to come over this impasse several scholars have suggested codification of Muslim Personal Law as a possible strategy to bring about reform within Muslim community. The current set of personal laws is not properly codified, which is why they are not easily comprehensible and there are abundant ambiguities. This is one of the reasons for their abuse by those with vested interests. Hence, codification of the entire gamut of Muslim Personal Laws should be given high priority. Citing the experience of enacting the Dissolution of Muslim Marriage Act, 1939, several scholars have pointed out that it would be possible to create a broad forum of legal scholars and Ulemas to lay ground for eventual codification (Engineer, 2005). BMMA have pursued the codification of Muslim Personal Law in consultations with various concerned groups and lawyers across the country with the objective of preparing a draft code that would then be placed before the Parliament. The attempt at codification has been criticized not only by outside groups such as the MWRN, but also internally in the BMMA. While agreeing that there is value in reclaiming the cultural category of "Muslim," and while supporting women's initiatives to reclaim their rights to religion and religious interpretation, many women activists are critical of codification. However, negotiations on codification based on the use of divergences in interpretation within various Islamic schools of thought cannot elicit all that the BMMA may want to achieve. So while, for instance, in the consultation held in Delhi in February 2012, there was agreement on limiting polygamy to the extent that the practice becomes impossibly difficult, the BMMA's demand that it be completely abolished was not met (Hasan, 2010). According to press reports, a group of Muslim scholars and activists have made a valiant attempt towards codification of Muslim Personal Law. The national consultation on codification has prepared a progressive draft, which among other things bans triple *talaq* and restricts polygamy. According to the reformist scholar Asghar Ali Engineer, the group is not bringing any new law but only reiterating the provisions which the Quran makes for Muslim men and women.

The other side of the story is that there is difference of opinion in regard to codification among the women networks all of those involved in fighting for Muslim women's rights say that their goal is to achieve gender equity under the law, there are some important differences of opinion among them. The question naturally arises whether all of those who use religious arguments in arguing for gender equity are truly convinced that Islam—when interpreted 'correctly'—can provide everything that women need. The choice of an Islamic discourse can be 'both genuine an expression of religious convictions—and a strategic attempt to acquire legitimacy that also serves to broaden the base of support for women's rights within the community. As pointed by Vatuk (2008) on the basis of her discussion with Noorjehan Safia Niaz, a Co-Director of WRAG, that, since there are some areas of Islamic law that are inherently biased against women, WRAG advocates taking what is relevant from the Quran while at the same time pressuring the state to codify Muslim law a new (as quoted in Vatuk 2008). Those who argue for reform from within the Muslim Personal Laws as the best strategy for enhancing the scope of Muslim women's rights ignore the fact that such an approach tends to freeze identities within religious boundaries. "So, we need to go outside it to provide women those rights as well. This is not to say that religious law should not be followed. But it is not enough" (MWRN activist to Kirmani 2009).

Here Moghadam's (2002) distinction between 'Islamic' and 'Muslim' feminists is relevant: the latter are 'believing women who agree that Islamization has been detrimental to women and approach issues of legal reform from that perspective, but also "often use familiar cultural concepts and religious phrases" in order to promote their reformist goals more effectively to a Muslim audience. However, there is little doubt that others sincerely believe that "Islam already provides women all the rights they could possibly require", some activists are of the opinion that "it is enough if women get the rights that they are given by Islam" (Vatuk, 2008; Kirmani, 2009a; Zaman, 2013).

These differences of opinion among the Muslim society have diluted the spirit of activism. This point has made it somewhat difficult for MWRN to keep its membership rolls intact and to present a united front towards the male religious establishment that most regard as their principal adversary in the battle for legal reform. But, thus far it has not led to a permanent cleavage. All of those involved seem to believe that more is to be gained from continuing to work together than from allowing their differences to derail the larger effort. Whereas those who resist going outside of *sharia* are naturally averse to state intervention in reform of MPL, they do not necessarily rule out supporting pro-woman legislation that impinges only indirectly upon their code of personal law.

Conclusion

Islamic feminist activism in India is not yet an organized 'social movement', in the strict sense of that term. It is being pursued by a rather amorphous assortment of individuals and groups, all engaged in avid discussion and debate about the negative impact of MPL on women but only loosely organized in terms of action. These women share similar goals—to spread awareness of 'the correct teachings of Islam' about women's rights (*huquq-e-niswan*) and find ways to help women gain practical access to them (Vatuk, 2008, Schneider, 2009). After analysing the vision and mission of different Muslim women rights organization and also understanding the fallout of Muslim Women Maintenance Act there has been overwhelming engagement of Muslim women activists over the question of changing the situation of Muslim women, which cannot be disassociated from the fact that her category is constructed through her community. Therefore, the first question which has haunted the Muslim community in India is how to change the situation of Muslim women, how to emancipate her from oppressive personal laws so that cases like Shah Bano, Imrana and Gudiya are not repeated and there are no more sacrifices of Muslim women on the alter of Muslim Personal Laws. These cases are clear evidence that process of reform is at standstill. One course can be for concerned Muslims to begin lobbying for codification of Muslim Personal Law. The other course can be to work for piecemeal reforms, taken upon a priority basis those provisions where the contradiction between the constitutional law and the personal law is severe or the law as understood and applied at present is clearly in dissonance with the principles of equity, justice and good conscience.

Undoubtedly codification can go a long way towards removing the existing contradiction between the Constitutional and Personal Laws as well as making them consonant with the principles of equity, justice and social conscience. A noted social scientist Imtiaz Ahmad (1994) has pointed out there are two catches in this, first codification is difficult. Yet, it may turn out on close led from the top often ends up creating unforeseen difficulties which are subsequently difficult to rectify. Second, codification can only follow emergence of an agreed upon draft code of Muslim Personal Law. Such an agreed upon code will present the same difficulties as those implicit in the rationalization and/or reform woman of specific provisions. Indeed, there is every possibility that the difficulties may be greater as the process of codification of their law may be seen by the community as a wholesale change of Muslim Personal Law against which a strong sentiment already exists. It may also be recalled that the reforms that took place in the 1930s were not concerned with gender justice but rather with the establishment of a more authentically "Islamic" social world for the community (Minault, 2009: 83; Metcalf, 2002: 2-3). Legal reform becomes tricky because the moral and legal framework on which it is based is supposed to be immutable. In addition, it is projected as an important issue for all Muslims because it supposedly defines their identity. Rather than focusing all energies on changing personal laws in one go, a piecemeal process, of reform promoting gender equality and justice will be the appropriate course, it would be more rewarding to make a small beginning and work towards an eventual codification of the entire corpus of Muslim personal law. The need of the moment accordingly is to build consensus across the community about the need for reform. Muslim women's activism needs to promote women's rights to enhance Muslim woman's situation based on the everyday experiences of Muslim women.

REFERENCES

Agnes, F. (N.D.) "From Shah Bano to Kausar Bano—Contextualizing the 'Muslim Woman' within a communalised polity". Retrieved from http://indiandemocracy08.berkeley.edu/docs/Agnes-From Shahbano2Kausar on 02/11/2015

Agnes, Flavia (1995). "Redefining the agenda of the women's movement within a secular framework", in Tanika Sarkar and Urvashi Butalia (eds.) *Women and Right-Wing Movement: Indian Experiences*. New Delhi: Kali for Women, pp. 136-157.

Agnes, Flavia (2002). "Transgressing Boundaries of Gender and Identity", *Economic and Political Weekly*, 37: 3695-3698.

Agnes, Flavia (2004). Women and Law in India: An Omnibus. New Delhi: Oxford University Press.

Ahmed, Imtiaz (1994). "Personal Laws: Promoting Reforms From Within", *Economic and Political Weekly*, pp. 2851-52.

Bacchetta, Paola (1994). "Communal Property/Sexual Property: On Representations of Muslim Women in a Hindu Nationalist Discourse", in Zoya Hasan (ed.) *Forging Identities: Gender, Communities and the State*. New Delhi: Kali for Women.

Butalia, Urvashi (2002). Confrontation and Negotiation: The Women's Movement's Response to Violence Against Women", in Karin Kapadia (ed.) *The Violence of Development: The Politics of Identity, Gender and Social Inequalities in India*. New Delhi: Kali for Women, pp. 207-234.

Engineer, Asghar Ali (ed.) (1995). *Problems of Muslim Women in India*. Hyderabad: Orient Longman.

Hasan, Zoya and Ritu Menon (2006). *Unequal Citizens: Socio-economic Status of Muslim Women in India*. Delhi: Oxford University Press.

Hasan, Zoya (1998). "Gender Politics, Legal Reform, and the Muslim Community in India", in Patricia Jeffery and Amrita Basu (eds.) *Appropriating Gender: Women's Activism and Politicized Religion in South Asia*. New York: Routledge, pp. 71-88.

Hasan, Zoya (2010). "Gender, Religion and Democratic Politics in India", *Third World Quarterly*, Vol. 31:6, pp. 939-954.

Hussain, Sabiha (2007). "Reflections on Islamic Identity, Citizenship Rights and Women's Struggle for Gender Justice: Illustration from India", *Journal of International Women's Studies*, 9:1, pp. 63-79.

Indian Express, (September 28, 2004)

Kazi, Seema (1999). *Muslim Women in India*. London: Minority Rights Group International.

Kirmani, Nida (2008) History, memory and localised constructions of insecurity. *Economic and Political Weekly*, 43(9), pp. 57-64.

Kirmani, Nida. 2009(a). Beyond the Religious Impasse: Mobilizing for Muslim Women's Rights in India, *Birmingham: Religions and Development*. Working Paper 35.

Kirmani, Nida (2009b) Deconstructing and reconstructing 'Muslim women' through women's narratives. *Journal of Gender Studies*, 18(1), pp. 47-62.

Kirmani, Nida (2011). "Beyond the Impasse: 'Muslim Feminism(s)' and the Indian Women's Movement", *Contributions to Indian Sociology*, 45:1, pp. 1-26.

Kishwar, Madhu (1998). *Religion at the Service of Nationalism,* Delhi: Oxford University Press.

Kumar, Radha (1993). *The History of Doing: An Illustrated Account of Movements for Women's Rights and Feminism in India, 1800-1990.* New Delhi: Zubaan.

Kumar, Radha (1994). "Feminism Faces Fundamentalism in India", *Agenda,* 21, pp. 81-92.

Lateef, Shahida (1990). *Muslim Women in India: Political and Private Realities 1890s-1980s,* London: Zed Books Ltd.

Law Commission Member Hails Syeda Acting 'Kazi' to Solemnize 'Nikah,' *One India News* (Aug. 14, 2008), http://news.oneindia.in/2008/08/14/law-commission-member-hails-syeda-acting-kazi-to-solemnise-nikah-1218717283.html.

Lazreg, Susan (1998). "Feminism and Difference: The Perils of Writing as a Woman on Women in Algeria", *Feminist Studies,* 14:1, pp. 81-107.

Mabro, Judy (1991). *Veiled Half-Truths: Western Travellers' Perceptions of Middle Eastern Women.* London: I.B. Taurus & Co. Ltd.

Mahmood, Tahir (1993). *Human Rights in Islamic Law.* Genuine Publications, New Delhi.

Mahmood, Tahir (1986) *Personal Laws in Crisis—Endowment Lectures,* Bombay University.

Menon, Nivedita (2011). "Introduction", in Nivedita Menon (ed.) *Gender and Politics in India,* Delhi: Oxford University Press.

Metcalf, Barbara Daly (2002). *Perfecting Women. Maulana Ashraf 'Ali Thanawi's Bihishti Zewar.* New Delhi: Oxford University Press.

Minault, Gail (2009). *Gender, Language and Learning. Essays in Indo-Muslim Cultural History.* Ranikhet: Permanent Black

Moghadam, Valentine (2002). Islamic Feminism and its Discontents: Toward a Resolution of the Debate. *Signs.* 27 (4): 1135-71

Mohanty, Chandra (1988). "Under Western Eyes: Feminist Scholarship and Colonial Discourses", *Feminist Review,* 30, pp. 61-88.

Nainar, V. (2000). *Muslim Women's Views on Personal Laws: The Influence of Socio-economic Factors.* Women's Research and Action Group, Bombay.

Omvedt, Gail (1993). *Reinventing Revolution: New Social Movements and the Socialist Tradition in India.* New York and London: M.E. Sharpe.

Rajan, Rajeswari Sunder (1998). "Is the Hindu Goddess a Feminist?", *Economic and Political Weekly,* 33: 44, pp. ws34-ws38.

Rajan, Rajeswari Sunder (2003). *The Scandal of the State: Women, Law, and Citizenship in Post-colonial India,* Delhi: Permanent Black.

Sachar Committee Report (2006). *Social, Economic and Educational Status of the Muslim Community of India.* Prime Minister's High Level Committee Cabinet Secretariat Government of India, pp. 19-20.

Sands, Kathleen (2008). "Feminisms and Secularisms", in Janet

Jakobsen and Ann Pellegrini (eds.) *Secularisms*, Durham, NC: Duke University Press, pp. 308-29.

Sarkar, Tanika, and Urvashi Butalia (eds.) (1995). *Women and Right-Wing Movement: Indian Experiences*, London: Zed Books Ltd.

Schneider, Nadja-Christina (2009). "Islamic Feminism and Muslim Women's Rights Activism in India: from Transnational Discourse to Local Movement. Or Vice Versa?", in: *Journal of International Women's Studies*, 11, 1: 56-71.

Sezgin,Yüksel, (2012), *Women's rights in the triangle of state, law, and religion: a comparison of Egypt and India*. http://www.themenplattform-ez.de/wp-content/uploads/2012/07/Women-in-the-triangle-of-Law-State-and-Religion-Egypt-and-India.pdf.

Spivak, Gayatri (1989). "In a Word: An Interview", *Differences*, 1, pp. 124-156.

Spivak, Gayatri (1990). *Postcolonial Critic: Interviews, Strategies, Dialogues*. New York: Routledge.

Spivak, Gayatri (1993). *Inside the Teaching Machine*. New York: Routledge.

Subramaniam, Mangala (2004). "The Indian Women's Movement", *Contemporary Sociology* (Special Issue: A Symposium: Bridging Scholarship: The Indian Women's Movement), 33:6, pp. 635-639.

Subramaniam, Mangala (2006). *The Power of Women's Organizing: Gender, Caste and Class in India*. Lanham, MD: Lexington Books.

Vatuk, Sylvia (2008). "Islamic Feminism in India: Indian Muslim Women Activists and the Reform of Muslim Personal Law", *Modern Asian Studies*, 42: 2-3, 489-518.

Yegenoglu, Meyda (2003). "Veiled Fantasies: Cultural and Sexual Difference in the Discourse of Orientalism", in Lewis, Reina and Mills, Sara (eds.) *Feminist Postcolonial Theory: A Reader*, Edinburgh: University of Edinburgh Press, pp. 542-566.

Zaman, Rafia (2013). "(Re)Framing the Issues: Muslim Women's Activism", *Contemporary India*, | January 013 Nr. 126, ASIEN, *The German Journal of Contemporary Asia*, pp. 26-47.

3

Gender, Conflict and Violence in Jammu & Kashmir

Abha Chauhan

Gender perspective in studies on conflict and violence has been largely ignored or subsumed by the wider political concerns. In conflict zones, as in the state of Jammu & Kashmir (J&K) in India, the state structures are often combined with exceeding militarism, fundamentalism and national chauvinism to reinforce patriarchal practices resulting in relegating women either invisible or to the periphery. This marginalization of women has precluded their engagement with authority and presence in important decision-making bodies leading to their views being ignored on the questions of conflict resolution, peace initiatives, demilitarization, reconstruction and similar issues.

The state of Jammu & Kashmir is located in the northwest part of India at the international border and the line of control mainly between India and Pakistan. The state occupies an area of 222,236 square kms. and a population of 12.55 million as per the 2011 census. It has three very diverse regions—Jammu, Kashmir and Ladakh. The Muslims constitute 68.3 per cent of the total population of the state, Hindus are 28.4 per cent, Sikhs 1.87 per cent, and Buddhists 1.1 per cent with a very few people of other religions. However, Hindus, Muslims and Buddhists are concentrated largely in Jammu, Kashmir and Ladakh respectively. The state is predominantly rural with 73 per cent population living in villages and 70 per cent people engaged in agriculture and allied sectors. The literacy rate is 67.17, with male literacy as 76.75 and female literacy as 56.43. The low literacy rate of women and the appalling sex-ratio of 889 suggest deteriorating status of women in the state (Jammu & Kashmir Profile 2011).

Jammu & Kashmir is unique in many ways. It is the only Muslim majority state in India, it enjoys special status under Article 370 of the Constitution of India, and it has its own Constitution (and flag) which came into force on 26th January, 1957. The genesis of its special status goes back to the time of India's partition (1947). The then ruler of Kashmir, Maharaja Hari Singh signed Instrument of Accession with India on 26th October, 1947 by which the princely state became a part of Indian Union (Samaddar, 2004). This conflicting situation was accelerated with the invasion by the tribal raiders from Pakistan side as well as some internal disturbances. As a result of this war, substantial area was taken over by Pakistan some of which was handed over to China. The territorial dispute somehow remained unresolved as both India and Pakistan continued to claim Jammu & Kashmir as its own. The conflict between them has persisted since then and led to subsequent wars over Kashmir (1965, 1971, 1999) as well as border tensions, firings and skirmishes that are continuing till date.

The state of J&K, particularly since last twenty five years or so, has seen increasing conflict and violence due to militarization of the region and terror of the militants, role of many sponsored Islamic fundamentalist and separatist groups, large scale migration of people from the Valley (mainly the Kashmiri Pandits), hardening of communal and regional identities, violations of civil and human rights, and straining of Centre-State relations along with the flouting of federal contracts. The state saw escalation of conflict where many people lost their lives or disappeared. All this impacted women and their agency in a significant manner—as persons, as citizens, as well as wives and mothers. Though women have faced violence as physical and sexual abuse, rape or displacement and forced migration, they have also played an active role in combating violence and conflict through resistance, peace and negotiations.

This chapter seeks to challenge the marginalization of women's representations in violent and conflict situations and the patriarchal project in which they are located. It argues for the presence of women and inclusion of gender sensitivity in many of the laws like those granting special powers to the police and the armed forces in 'disturbed areas', to counter the imbalance produced due to militarized and masculinised state structures.

The analysis is based on the candid discussions and interviews with women (20) affected by conflict in Kashmir prior to the 2014 J&K assembly elections and much before the present crises started in July 2016 in Kashmir. Women respondents are from varied socio-economic backgrounds, and of all age groups belonging to different districts of Kashmir division. Their views on social movement, political activism and participation, the role of armed forces, conflict resolution and peace building, particularly related to their involvement since 1990 have been analyzed. The identities of these women have been protected by not giving their names though a few well known ones are mentioned as they openly express their views in media and also and had no objection.

Political Activism and Social Movement

In the late eighties, the wind of *azadi* (freedom) started blowing in the region, and many young men crossed over the border to Pakistan side of Kashmir and joined militant groups to get training to fight the Indian Government and Indian forces including the army, Central Reserve Police Force (CRPF), Border Security Force (BSF) etc. This movement for freedom of Kashmir or what is popularly known as *tehreek* which started in Kashmir around 1989 reached its peak in mid 1990s. Meanwhile, the militant groups like the Jammu and Kashmir Liberation Front (JKLF) gave up the armed struggle and forged a united political platform, 'All Party Hurriyat Conference' (APHC) in 1995 that occupied political space and legitimacy among people of Kashmir. Though the Assembly elections of 1996 and also of 2002 and 2008 reflected the changed mood of people towards democracy, the feeling of alienation among them did not end and voices of separatists continued to be heeded. Much of the resentment among people was with the armed forces and later on renegades (*Ikwanis*) due to the treatment at their hands and violation of human rights.

Many people have died, killed or disappeared in more than two decades of conflict. Kashmiris estimate it to be about 100,000 civilian deaths. Many children were orphaned and large number of women became widows or 'half widows'. The widows were of those people who were either killed by the terrorists or widows of militants or those whose spouses were killed in the cross firing. The number of widows in J&K registered with the Department of Social Welfare, J&K Government is 54,000. It is estimated that there are 129,600 widows and 226,800 orphans living in Kashmir who belong to ex-militants and civilians killed in the armed conflict. It follows that an estimated number of 8,842 per year and 737 per month widows and orphans were added to the total during the past twenty years or so (Dabla, 2009). Another estimate puts the total number of widows in J&K as 196,604 (India Current Affairs, 2010). The state government pays a meagre Rs. 200 per month to widows, destitute and handicapped persons in the Valley under the Integrated National Security Scheme.

Conflict in Kashmir: Participation in *Tehreek*

At the time of *tehreek* almost every person and every part of Kashmir in some way or the other were involved and affected. In nearly all the towns and villages, majority of families had men who were a part of the movement. People were supportive of it in various ways. Euphoria was generated whereby supporting the *tehreek* and actions of *Mujahids* (crusader, fighter in the way of *Allah*) were seen prestigious. The general view was that the *tehreek* people were respected for their bravery and did not harm any fellowmen and their community and village members. Many girls got married to *tehreek* persons those days. The opinions about *Mujahids* were very positive in the beginning of *tehreek*. It was said that they never made forceful entries into homes or engaged in sexual assaults, harassment or any kind of exploitation.

It was admitted by many people that from nearly all the houses some or the other member crossed the border to get the training. This was around 1989-1991. Many of them were from humble background and were easily swayed. It also emerged from these conversations that in general women and old people did not encourage their sons and husbands or any other male relatives to go for such trainings. In fact, many times they did not approve of it also. The reasons given were like—who would like to lose their loved ones, or put their lives in danger? Some other interviewees however, felt that though people supported *tehreek* whole heartedly, they were afraid to acknowledge it.

The responses of many women suggest that besides the feeling of general apathy among people, the role of separatists, religious leaders, militants and support from across the border were important incentives. Some people yearned for revenge and revolt increased by the counselling and persuasion of trained persons in *tehreek*. It had an impact on youth psyche and many crossed over the line of control and got training for two years or more. It also shows that after initial enthusiasm, people started disassociating themselves with the *tehreek*. Various factors were responsible for this change. One was ruthless crushing of the movement by the security forces and the other was the entry of foreign militants and decline of the role of local militants and separatist leaders. It was difficult to distinguish between a true *Mujahid* and a fake one, as someone said.

In the beginning it is said that the movement was popular as local separatist leaders and organizations were involved. The Jammu and Kashmir Liberation Front (JKLF), the armed militant group wanted independent Kashmir for all Kashmiris—Muslims and Pandits. But slowly with the intervention of militant groups like Allah Tigers and hardening stand of women's groups as Dukhtarane Millat (daughters of the faith, DM) and Muslim Khawateen Markaz (MKM), the movement took Islamic colour and imposition of specific religious identity for women began to be imposed. Though that time, this diktat was rejected by most of the girl students in Kashmir as it was somewhat possible to resist imposition of community identity in the earlier period of struggle, it became almost impossible with worsening of the situation (Manchanda, 2001: 58; Suri, 2011: 13-14). The divide between the Muslims and Kashmiri Pandits began to widen, the *Kashmiriyat* started declining, the atmosphere got vitiated and some of the prominent Pandits were killed. This led to the mass exodus of Pandits on 19-20 January, 1990. Appeals were made to Kashmiri women to show their allegiance as members of a particular religious and ethnic community.

Views of Women Respondents on the Violence by Armed Forces

The army posts came up in or nearby every village as soon as the movement spread and men crossed over the border. They were at the range of 2-5 kms. from their homes. Almost all the respondents had negative views about the army and security forces. They not only blamed them for crackdowns, interrogation humiliation and beating, but their very presence made women apprehensive, insecure and restricted. The stories of harassment and torture abound and perhaps there was hardly a family in Kashmir which did not go through such experiences. This was more with the families having *Mujahid* or those suspected to be having one. Besides those directly involved, there were also those who were indirectly related to the *Mujahid* in some way or the other. At a few times there were only suspects and all this led to unnecessary troubling people who in turn picked up guns and became *Mujahids*.

A respondent **A** (67) of village Ongam in Bandipora said since the Army was stationed at about 2 kilometres from her house its personnel used to come many times. They gutted her house at night twice with gun powder for the reason that two of her sons were involved in militancy. They always talked in abusive language and had no respect for women, according to her. One of the women **Z** (65) of Arwani, Bijbehara, district Anantnag whose two sons (aged 31 and 28) were killed in encounter with Indian army and by an unidentified gunmen respectively in 1997 said that during the times her sons used to be militants there were frequent night raids and harassment of the family members which also continued after their martyrdom.

Those days searches, frisking and thrashing by Army was common, particularly of those who were *Mujahideen* or linked to groups like Hizb-ul-Mujahideen or Lashkar-e'Toiba. During raid armed forces also stole valuables as reported by some. According to them, army did not spare even women and girls while abusing or beating them. There were cases of teasing, stone throwing and passing of lewd remarks by them when girls and women passed nearby their locations or when the army men happened to pass the village. There are also instances of sexual assaults and rape during interrogations and crackdowns.

Y (50) of Pohru Goorpur, Pulwama had four daughters and two sons. One of her sons crossed the border in 1990 and came back after training as a renowned militant after two years. He was caught by STF (Special Task Force) personnel one day and interrogated badly. From that day onwards, she never saw her son. Armed forces used to raid her house daily in order to arrest him and beat all the in-mates ruthlessly. The whole village was harassed mentally and physically. Her husband and another son were arrested although they were not militants. **X** (60) of Niwhatta in Srinagar had somewhat similar story to tell. Her only son (23) was killed by the security forces Rashtriya Rifles (RR) even though he was not a militant according to her. She is left with three daughters now.

The link between war and control of women's sexuality and reproduction is clearly visible. In Kashmir, rape has been used as a weapon to punish, intimidate, force and degrade by security forces as well as armed militants (Global Report on Women's Human Rights, 1998). It has been used as an individual as well as collective form of punishment like those committed by the security forces in Pazipora (1990), Kunana Poshpara (1991), Chak Saidpora (1992), Theno Budpathery Kangan (1994) and Wavoosain Srinagar (1997). Many incidents of torture and beating of women were reported during the discussion. Some cases of rape and sexual harassment also came to light.

Tabinda Gani of Langate, Handwara in district Kupwara was studying in class VIII and was just 13 year old when she was raped and killed by four men while coming back from school in 2007. Two of the accused were locals and two others were from different states. The daughter and daughter-in-law (pregnant) of one of the respondents from Bandipora, **B** (60) were raped by security forces. According to her, this happened when the army came to their house in search of her militant son and could not find him. They got angry and tortured and raped the two women. Later, her *Mujahid* son was killed in an encounter with army. Her second son was kidnapped by Ikhwanis and was killed and his dead body was found nearby river. After that her husband was arrested many times by army finally killed by Ikhwanis and his body too was thrown into water. She herself was beaten many times and abused by the army, according to her.

Another important reason that can be discerned from these interactions is the emergence of a counter force by army of surrendered militants, the renegades, known as *Ikhwani*s against *Mujahids*. They were more ruthless knowing well the language of the people and the topography of the region. Javed Shah and Kuka Parry are such examples of *Ikhwanis* who looted and exploited Kashmiris and killed them, according to some interviewees. Even the foreign militants did not spare them and looted the house.

The story of the respondent **A** (67) of Ongam, Bandipora town is the most heart rending one. She lost her husband and four sons during the conflict, of the remaining two, one was hit by bullet in his leg and became handicap, and the other was brutally tortured by army and became unfit. Even after a gap of 15 years of the disappearance of her son the state unit of Police from Bandipora is still harassing and abusing her demanding the appearance of her disappeared son. She is frequently called to the Police Station Bandipora like a history sheeter which makes her feel quite humilated, she said.

Therefore, the situation was a complicated one where attack and counter-attack became the order of the day. Besides this many people disappeared. They were picked up from homes or called to the camps or stations and never came back. On the whole, many people felt disillusioned after a few years of turmoil.

One of the women, **U** (43) from Kralapora, district Bandipora was tortured by the army as they thought she is a woman militant. Her husband, a militant like others did not surrender, but became *shaheed* (martyr) according to her. She was interrogated for supporting *tehreek* and then lodged in central jail in Srinagar. At that time nobody came to her help or provided any support. Then her parents approached the court and she was released from jail after 3 months.

Some peace was seen returning during the intermediary periods as militants surrendered, shelling reduced at the ceasefire line and foreign mercenaries tracked back. The elections to panchayats (2001, 2011) and to the State Assembly (2009) further tried to make the atmosphere better as people participated in significant numbers despite the threats from militants. However, the alienation and disenchantment never ceased and erupted time and again at every appropriate situation. In 2008, the Amarnath land row acquired a huge dimension wherein perhaps for the first time, a large number of people in Jammu agitated against what they call the 'Kashmir-centric' policy of the government. The state government under the pressure of separatists supported by people at large withdrew its decision to transfer 99 acres of forest land to the Amarnath Shrine Board in the Kashmir valley to set up temporary shelters and facilities for Hindu pilgrims. This led to strong protest and opposition with unprecedented violence in Jammu region and the state remained in the grip of turmoil for at least 3-4 months.

In Kashmir, the Shopian case in 2009 called for mass opposition when two girls who were sisters-in-law, Nilofer and Asiya were abducted, raped and murdered under mysterious circumstances. The villagers and the local people alleged that this was done by the security forces. In 2010 there was a strong protest in Kashmir against the fake encounter at Machil. Almost 300 people got killed during these three years (2008-10). In 2010 alone nearly 120 people were killed most of them young and engaged in pelting stones. Protests continued for about 6 months and there was curfew for almost 3 months continuously.

Though some women respondents came out in support of the protests and enthusiastically participated in them, most of them said they were not so active now. They however, supported them and were shocked and angry, particularly at the Shopian case. Some women respondents lost their young children in the 2010 encounter, most of them during firing without any fault. The son (22) of **T** (55) from Bijbehara, district Anantnag was shot dead in the afternoon during the month of Ramadan when he was going to the hospital to see his friend. The general opinion about the army being the enemy continued, and got reinforced with the incidents in 2009 and 2010. Amidst all this, the debates regarding withdrawal or continuation of Acts like 'Armed Forces (Special Powers) Act' (AFSPA) went on.

The *Armed Forces (Special Powers) Act* (AFSPA) passed on September 11, 1958 by the Parliament of India is a law with six sections granting special powers to the armed forces in what the Act terms as 'disturbed areas'. These are the north eastern states of Arunachal Pradesh, Assam, Manipur, Tripura, Meghalaya, Mizoram and Nagaland. It was implemented in 1990 in the state of Jammu and Kashmir (3.5 lakh army personnel) for counter-insurgency operations as the *Armed Forces (Jammu and Kashmir) Special Powers Act, 1990*. The Act has been at the heart of debate about human rights violations in the regions of its enforcement, where arbitrary killings, torture, cruel, inhuman and degrading treatment and enforced disappearances have happened.

The United Nations human rights organizations such as 'Amnesty International' and 'Human Rights Watch' and several individuals have criticized the Act (AFSPA) and its abuse in Kashmir. The army on the other hand supports the Act in J&K state with the plea that four hundred or more terrorists are present in the state and there continues violation of ceasefire at the borders with the ongoing infiltration of the terrorists. The separatists criticize this stand of Army and leaders of ruling and some opposition parties and support the phasing out of the Act. People in Kashmir in general, including women are very much against the AFSPA.

Public Political Participation and Women's Agency

The discussions and interactions with women reveal that though they have often succumbed to the pressures and willingly accepted their roles and participated in the movement, they have also negotiated in the face of conflict and worked out strategies of resistance and opposition. It shows their capacity to move beyond victimhood to agency. This was seen in their various 'stretched' roles when grieving mothers sacrificed their sons and transformed the mother as agency taking their private grief into public space and politicizing it through groups like the 'Association of Parents of Disappeared Persons' (Manchanda, 2001).

Similarly in other studies like on the anti-Sikh riots, Veena Das (1986) explores how the widows of the Delhi carnage took the symbols of mourning and pollution and gave them a political meaning in defiance of the authorities who wanted them to terminate their mourning. Paula Banerjee's essay (2001) explores the grey zone between victimhood and agency in the study of conflict in Assam and Nagaland through the testimonies of women supporters of the insurgency movement on the one hand, and the work of women's peace groups, on the other.

A more recent work by Urvashi Butalia (2002) is related to women's voices from Kashmir. These are voices not just of victims but also of those playing different roles from caretakers to participants or from combatants to peacemakers. The essays in the volume bring out in their own ways the fear, the loss, the personal scars, the pain, and the techniques of survival in different situations of agony. In our study also one finds a constant interplay of structures and agency where the actions of the women were constrained by the intersectionalities of patriarchy, class, religion and educational status among others. These case studies thus explore those areas, which traditionally remained male dominant domains and were devoid of gender perspective.

A woman (67) respondent **A** of Bandipora district attends 'Association of Parents of Disappeared Persons' (APDP) meeting regularly on 10th day of every month in Pratap Park in Srinagar where she has registered missing report of two of her disappeared sons. In that meeting everyone is treated equally and given the same respect as all are going through the same experience. There are some women who are close to Hurriyat even if at times they are critical of them. The respondent **B** (60) also of Bandipora district is not a member of any political party but she joins protests against India and has supported Hurriyat initiatives and participated actively even during 2008 Amarnath land row. Then she became highly dissatisfied with them and did not protest in the Shopian incident in 2009 though she feels very much for Nelofar and Asiya and has experienced similar situation at her home.

Having lost their dear ones, women respondents feel that the sacrifices were not worth it. According to **A,** only those people are happy these days who brainwashed 'our' children to cross LOC and their own children are in other countries where they are settled along with their families. They only grabbed money in the name of *Jihad* and looted everything here. In those days they were known as pious men who will help to give freedom from India. But they turned out to be *dalal* (brokers) who sold Kashmir to Pakistan and India for their own interests. Today the respondent **U** who participated in the protests but was not helped by the Hurriyat leaders when she was in jail, feels that they gave them guns for their own interests. The disillusionment with the Hurriyat and the other separatist leaders, who could not capitalize on the opportunity and fill in the void created by dismantling of state institutions and structures, was visible with most of the interviewees. Some of them, however, still have faith in them. Most of them seem to be due to poverty rather than the genuine concern for movement.

A young woman **C** (29) from the Bandipora district said that she is a member of Hurriyat Conference (G) and 'our duty is to participate in protests. Educated and women from upper castes did not participate in protests because they have enough resources like government jobs and lands to support their families. As we poor have no other source of income we are ready to take money for protests.' She also said that in 2008 during Amarnath land agitation they were given Rs. 200/- per protest by Hurriyat

Conference to protest against India. In 2009 when Shopian case happened she protested against India but at that time money was given only to special women, to those who are in Hurriyat from last 20 years. In 2010 she participated but was not given any money.

Some women are leaders in their own right doing their own bit, even if not joining any political or militant outfit. One of them **D** from Srinagar (61), a highly educated woman has formed an organization for the rehabilitation of women and children. The organization is working for education of orphaned children, empowerment of the widows and the underprivileged women, and their health care. She feels that in some ways conflict has empowered women and given space to them (like her) to come out into the field and start their own work. Another highly educated woman **E** (66), also from Srinagar remained associated with a Delhi NGO which started peace education and brought women together in many intra-Kashmir conferences. A vocal and bold woman leader **F** (51) from Srinagar is one of the founder leaders of a party called 'Muslim Khawateen Markaz' (MKM) and has been active with other separatist organizations. Before that after being released from prison, she started the organization 'Association for Families of Kashmiri Prisoners' (AFKP) because she saw the pathetic condition in which their prisoners and their families lived.

Parveena Ahangar (59), about whom everyone knows, a resident of Gangboo, Srinagar is a President of 'Association of Parents of Disappeared Persons' (APDP) formed in 1994. APDP works for finding those who disappeared from their homes and their whereabouts are not known even till today. The state government claims that they have joined militant groups and have crossed over the border (they have a list of 2,338 such men) but their families do not agree with this. They have seen hard times and continue to do so, running from pillar to post to the police stations, courts etc. to get information about their husbands, sons or brothers. A more recent report released by the APDP in August 2011, entitled 'Half Widow, Half Wife—Responding to Gendered Violence in Kashmir' provides a gender analysis of situation of half widows as well as of the larger security situation in Kashmir, and states that there are at least 1,500 half widows in J&K (Suri, 2011: 8-10).

Ending Violence, Conflict Resolution and Peace Building

Women are often marginalized in the discussion on conflict resolution and peace building processes as the violence comes to an end. Nevertheless, they have their own views pertaining to the issues. Most of them would like to play an important role in peace building processes. While talking to them, it appeared that many of them want independent Jammu and Kashmir or independent Kashmir free from India, neither a part of India nor of Pakistan. Some, however, said being Muslims they would like to be with Pakistan. A few also said that first India should free Kashmir and then we will decide what to do next.

According to the respondent **A** (67) resolution of Kashmir should be independence from India and Pakistan, but it is not possible as far as Pakistan is infiltrating through different routes and as far as India is sending more forces to Kashmir. Another woman **G** (43) from the same district similarly feels that India and Pakistan have no right to decide their future and the resolution of Kashmir is possible only when people of Kashmir become a part of the dialogue process on the issue. For them so far, Kashmir issue is more important than that of women.

Some respondents feel that for people of Kashmir, India and Pakistan are the same, they are the two sides of the same coin. The husband of **H** (50) of village Sonawar in Bandipora district was killed by the Militants and her sister-in-law's son by Army according to her. She, therefore, does not wish to go with either India or Pakistan. She feels that there is only one political resolution for this part of Kashmir and AJK (Azad Jammu and Kashmir)—independence or self-rule and women will have an important role in that resolution. Some of them like **B** (60) and C (29) would like to be with Pakistan and follow Islamic law and feel that Kashmir should be an integral part of it. This is because they are Muslims and do not want to live with *Kafirs* (non-Muslims).

The issue must be resolved peacefully taking into consideration the wishes of Kashmiri people, feels **I** (55) of Ganderbal district. If Kashmiris want to stay with Pakistan they must be given a chance to live with them—with the Muslim brothers. There are a few women like **J** (45) and **K** (46) of Ganderbal district who think that Independence should be granted to Jammu and Kashmir as soon as possible. However, they themselves do not want to be part of any resolution process and believe that women are not meant for politics and should not contribute politically. A clear difference emerged between the educated, urban middle or upper-middle class women and rural, poor and illiterate women regarding the views on resolution of Kashmir issue as well as on the role of women in politics. Both **J** (45) and **K** (46) are illiterate women living in the villages and they see freedom of Kashmir as the only solution with women playing no role in active politics.

Similarly, **I** (55) of Ganderbal district and **B** (60) of Bandipora district look at the future of Kashmir with Pakistan just because it is an Islamic country, though they know very well its role in instigating Kashmiri people to take up arms. They clearly blame India and security forces for their conditions and seem to have internalized the patriarchal and ethno-religious views which they believe to be true. On the other hand, educated women presented more balanced view, perhaps a workable solution, though their anger and disenchantment were no less. A woman activist **E** (66, Ph.D.) of Srinagar is of the view that India, Pakistan and Kashmiris, the three stake holders should sit together and talk about it and whatever is achievable should be decided. Women should be a part of this resolution. Another respondent of Srinagar **L** (59, Ph.D.) of Sanantnagar, Srinagar said that Kashmir problem can only be resolved by sitting at the table and having dialogue. Pakistan, India and Kashmir all three have to sit together and find a solution and they have to be very flexible. Women have to play a very important role in this, according to her.

For Parveena Ahangar, the issue is not of Kashmir, but one of finding those who are missing like her own son for which APDP is already making untiring efforts. She is determined not to let her hard work go waste. She is of the view that the Indian handling of Kashmir is a total disaster and Pakistan too had played an important role in keeping the issue alive. She wants them to leave it to the Kashmiris to resolve their own issues and not to interfere in their problems. The respondent **D** (61, Graduate) expressed the views that the problem can be resolved by talking to each other and not getting at each other's throat. Let the voices of Kashmiris reach both the countries India and Pakistan. A Kashmiri Pandit woman **M** (70), a doctor in Srinagar feels that they have to be friends with Pakistan and India and Pakistan should live like

America and Canada. For **F** (51, Graduate), the resolution of the Kashmir problem lies first in India accepting that Kashmir is a disputed territory. Then the other steps would come. The UN resolutions, aspirations of people are all important. Women, she feels can play a very important role. Ultimately, Kashmiris want *Azadi* which means pre-1947 Kashmir, according to her.

It must, however, be emphasized that educational level does not always go with having a less radical opinion as was seen with the views of **N** (50, Post-graduate), President, Dukhtaran-e-Millat a highly educated woman, but who does not even believe that Kashmir is part of India and who would like Muslim women to live under strict Islamic codes. The *tehreek* according to her is not the condition of turmoil, but a freedom struggle. For her, the solution to the Kashmir problem lies in one word which is "Plebiscite". India should agree that Kashmir is a disputed territory and have to give the Kashmiri Muslims their right to self-determination so that Kashmir problem is solved. The Kashmiris want freedom from India and then they will decide if they will go with Pakistan or establish an Islamic country of Kashmir, according to her.

Most of the women, however, said that they want peace and end of violence, though they wish for independent Jammu & Kashmir. Maximum widows have not remarried. They would like to give their children good education and improve their job prospects. Some, however, like Parveena see their role as members of organizations and associations to fight for their cause of finding disappeared children and men.

Conclusion

A gendered analysis of conflict and conflict-related violence has provided and given insights into the other forms of structural inequalities that came to exist in Kashmiri society. Traditionally, as a legacy of Rishi-Sufi cultural heritage women in Kashmir enjoyed more freedom and better status. Most of the women, except some orthodox upper-class Syed families did not wear *burqa* (veil). Women participated actively in economic activities like agriculture, animal husbandry and handicrafts. Women have been working side by side with men as agricultural wage labourers in rural areas and in cities as helpers in the families of potters, milk and vegetable vendors. Both in rural and urban areas, there was social acceptability of women working outside the home (Dabla, 1999). Today also they are seen in the market selling fish, vegetables and doing other works. However, on the whole a gendered division of labour was largely practiced and preferred in a patriarchal society.

Nearly all respondents agreed that women have been excluded from power, politics and decision-making processes. They were seen to be representatives of their community and religious identity. They embody community honour and bear the mark of their communal identity like veiling which became more pronounced in conflict situations. Many of them also admitted that though they are concerned about the Kashmir issue, they are not interested in politics and keep themselves away from such initiatives. Besides this, the general lack of interest in politics, their disillusionment with the political parties and leaders and their health condition were reasons for this attitude. An overall fatigue of waging long and relentless struggle with little gains seems to have taken a toll for a large number of women.

Women's experiences of conflict and violence are not homogeneous, but contextual and shifting. In Kashmir, women actively supported armed conflict in the beginning. When *tehreek* began in Kashmir in 1989-90, there was a mass support for the movement. It has already been noted how people in general and women in particular came out to support the movement, praised the *Mujahids,* assisted them to cross over the border for arms training and lent all possible help. Some of the reluctant women's voices of apprehension and concern for security and safety of the sons, brothers and husbands died in the general euphoria of enthusiasm and excitement of getting freedom from India and living in an independent Kashmir nation.

The number of women as active participants and supporters has declined since 1989-90. The dream of *Azadi* could not become true. People in general lost trust in those whom they believed will give them independence. The Hurriyat and other separatist leaders have lost their sheen. Except for a few, most women have no faith in them. Those who support are mainly from poor families and they suffered the most. The roles of army and security forces at many places were condemnable, the renegades or the *Ikhwanis* were used by army as informers for their own purposes. But militants also got the upper hand towards the end of the movement and people were actually caught in between the two. The violation of ceasefire and firing from across the border still continue.

The women respondents for most of the time appeared to be grieving mothers of their dead or missing sons and widows and 'half-widows' of their husbands who were killed and disappeared. They faced violence as they were beaten, tortured, teased and molested. But they also confronted, fought, searched, and formed associations and organizations for their cause. They proved themselves to be participants, survivors, risk-takers, activists and leaders. Their experiences are full of examples of their taking on to the armed forces, militants, running to police stations, getting FIR recorded, and pleading for the release of their sons or husbands.

As men avoided arrests, hid inside the houses and came at home secretly, women came out to protect and defend them at the cost of their lives and risk of their honour and security. They came out and created activism as violent conflict opened up the public space for women that was earlier controlled by men. Besides this some women resorted to speak the language of separatists and militants, insinuated by religion and nationalism. The 'Dukhtarane Millat' (DM) and 'Muslim Khawateen Markaz' (MKM) were such groups evolved in the course of time inspired by Islamic social reform activism. They seized the space created by the void of other organized protests and were in forefront of all campaigns. Their views during conflict thus remained curtailed by an Islamized identity in denial of the liberalism of Kashmiriyat cultural identity. The women occupied space with categorization as martyrs' mothers or raped women with largely limited and circumscribed agency.

Asiya Andrabi (50), the leader of DM was most active as her *burqa* brigade would rush out at her call to join any demonstration against the excesses by security forces. However, due to coercive and forceful tactics, many of the initiatives of these organizations like throwing acid on non-*burqa* clad women were not welcomed and in the course of time they became sidetracked and marginalized. Hurriyat itself did not provide sufficient space to women to lead the movement which resulted in their limited involvement. A powerful woman leader **F** (51) of Muslim Khawateen Markaz laments of being used as a woman in the movement. She said that when the Hurriyat came into existence they gave a public call for all social-human-religious organizations to join Hurriyat so that it becomes a platform from which this issue can be taken up. But, she was soon disillusioned as she realized that women's issues do not figure anywhere despite the fact that they participate in the movement actively.

However, there are some women like Parveena Ahangar who translated their private and personal grief of the sorrowing mother into public domain leading to the transformation of the mother as agency through her organization APDP. Women like **D** (61) have made their own contribution in taking steps towards bringing peace in the conflict-torn state by establishing organization for the rehabilitation of women and children, their education and health among other things. Even respondent **E** (66) who has been associated with the Delhi NGO for quite some time now feels that the present movement has empowered women to a certain extent because for one or the other reason they came out into the streets.

The views on conflict giving women empowerment thus remain partial, though significant. The respondent **M** (70), a qualified doctor and a Kashmiri Pandit woman who chose to stay in Kashmir during the period of turmoil, feels that it is difficult to say that 'we've been empowered with diktats coming out every day', but she is happy that women are coming out in big numbers and they are doing well. On the same question, **N** (50) too feels that the question is not so much of empowerment, but of the realization that the Kashmiri women have certain rights and responsibilities that they needed to fulfil, and that they could not be a mere spectator anymore.

However, women themselves see their activity as non-political and an extension of their domestic concerns, i.e. the traditional roles of nurturing and protective mother. Women's activism in conflict flows from their everyday concerns of keeping the family together and so are their initiatives towards reconciliation and peace-making. Women forged survival strategies, built dialogues, developed co-existence and reconciliation at the grassroots level, but got marginalized when formal politics took over at the negotiating table.

The absence of autonomous and secular women's organizations and groups in Kashmir limited the space for women's independent activism and the possibility of transcending the communalization of the struggle. The groups like DM and MKM got marginalized in the process as they handled the issue in a sectarian and pro-militant and pro-Pakistan manner rather than making it independent and putting the concern of women at the centre of all issues. Before they realized, it became too late. The self-interest of the people was expressed as the national interest which is Kashmir nation—an independent entity, separate from India.

There is a general apathy with the militant groups as well as the separatists. The sympathy, faith, respects and pride through which the earlier *Mujahids* were looked at has given way to doubt, uncertainty and disdain in many cases. Though some people still feel empathy towards the Mujahids and militants and are forced to believe in them, their situation is one of ambivalence and mixed feeling. Some women, like Asiya Andrabi consider them nationalists and freedom fighters. Their trust in the independent Kashmir is unshaken. Women are aware of their unequal situation in society and in the movement, but they prefer to negotiate from that position and evolve their own strategies than to make their protests known. They feel that the Indian state is unjustly and forcefully trying to integrate people who were independent and they have to support their own people for the cause of Kashmiri nationalism.

Most of the women have been sufficiently indoctrinated on religious lines in which the gender division of labour is well inscribed in family and society which make them supportive of their own power structure. The state interventionists role and the armed intrusions impose further patriarchal structures that tend to legitimize the masculine and hierarchical nature of their own religion and society and therefore, supportive of the idea of Kashmiri nationalism and peace coming only after independence. For women in Kashmir, peace will come with independence and will also mean development and growth. In the process of struggle, women do not feel completely marginalized and hence still not appropriated by the state but continue to provide sustainability to the movement. Unlike in some other parts of conflict-ridden places like in the North-east, women in Kashmir have not been able to build independent Kashmir Peace Groups.

Despite the similarities of opinions with men, with their society, religion and nation, the women's voices come out quite distinctly in this study—whether during conflict or any form of violence, at the time of negotiation or on the questions of resolution and peace-making. In every situation, women have borne the maximum brunt of something chosen and decided by the others. The definition of conflict resolution and peace for them would definitely mean resolving of Kashmir issue, but it does not mean living in the condition as they are doing today under the multiple burdens of violence and conflict, coming from military, militancy and masculinity, class, religion, gender, poverty and illiteracy.

It can thus be said that violent and conflict situations impact women's lives considerably, especially those living under oppressive patriarchal structures sanctioned by customs and religious orthodoxy. It brings out the differential construction and contestation by women in situations of violence and conflict and the steps they have taken in building peace. This study not only brings the question of gender centre-stage in the studies on violence, conflict and peace, but also creates a different kind of methodology that takes into account women experiences in their own voices, through methods like oral history and personal narratives. It also highlights that women need not be always seen as victims of violence and conflict but as initiators and negotiators with agency of their own.

REFERENCES

Banerjee, Paula (2001). "Between Two Armed Patriarchies: Women in Assam and Nagaland", in Rita Manchanda, ed., *Women, War and Peace in South Asia*. New Delhi: Sage.

Butalia, Urvashi (ed.) (2002). *Speaking Peace: Women's Voices from Kashmir*. New Delhi: Kali for Women.

Dabla, B.A. (2009). "Widows and Orphans in Kashmir". *The Daily: Rising Kashmir*. September, 20.

Das, Veena (1986). "Our Work to Cry, Your Work to Listen", in Veena Das, ed., *Mirrors of Violence; Communities, Riots and Survivors in South Asia*. New Delhi: Oxford University Press.

Human Rights Watch (1998). *Global Report on Women's Human's Rights, "Rape in Kashmir"*. New Delhi: Oxford University Press.

India Current Affairs (2010). "Status of Widow, Divorced and Deserted Women". *Women's Issues*. (Posted on 14.08.10).

Jammu and Kashmir Profile (2011). *Censusinfo India 2011*. Final Population Totals.

Manchanda, Rita (2001). "Guns and Burqa: Women in the Kashmir Conflict", in Rita Manchanda, ed., *Women, War and Peace in South Asia*. New Delhi: Sage.

Samaddar, Ranabir (ed.). (2004) *Peace Studies: An Introduction to the Concept, Scope and Themes*. New Delhi: Sage Publications.

Suri, Kavita. (2011). *Voices Unheard: Women, Conflict and Kashmir*. New Delhi: Shubhi Publications.

4

Individuality as 'Capability Deprivation'

A Critical Analysis in the Context of Women and Development in India

Hriday Ranjan Kalita and *Jyoti Prasad Saikia*

The word 'individuality' evokes two different impressions. First one is singularity, that we are talking about one particular human being who is a member of some group. The second impression is of distinctiveness, which suggests that a person has been able to develop a distinct identity of his or her own. In this second sense, the term individuality has been used in the western society. The very idea of individuality is a western concept, which has been borrowed by Indian society from western culture and it is as sudden and abrupt in terms of its appearance in the Indian society like many other 'adoptions' from the west. Hence, the Indian 'individual' is not a product of Indian culture per say. Amartya Sen has called poverty 'capability deprivation' as it deprives people of the capabilities to fulfil various needs. If, in reality, an 'individual' woman cannot be free to think and act for herself; is she 'capable' of attaining the benefits of 'development'? Focusing on this question, this research paper has tried to critically examine the state of 'individuality' in India as a factor responsible for creating 'capability deprivation' of women, impeding her ability to benefit from 'development'.

The concept of development has captivated the hearts and minds of theorists, thinkers, politicians and policy makers alike during the last few decades. Although, for many, especially the post-development thinkers, 'development' has 'failed'; for many 'third world' countries development is still very much alive and kicking. For them, the dream of development was such a beautiful one that they have decided to linger on a little bit more even though they have realised that it was just a dream. Resultantly, instead of formulating their own variants of development according to the specific needs and the contextual realities; they are still holding on to the concept of development as it was decades ago. The approaches, however, have certainly changed. One significant change in the development practice is the alleviation of women into the central stage. Women, as has been realised by the state, thinkers, theoreticians and policy makers, have become an indispensable part of the scheme for achieving development. It was Ester Boserup's pioneering work, 'Women's Role in Economic Development' which initiated this realisation (Boserup, 1970). The result of this realisation is an explicit worldwide emphasis on women, improvement of their condition and preparing them as resources for the process of development. India is not different in this context.

Inclusion of women in the agenda of development gave way to the rise of empowerment perspective in India in the decade of 1990s. Empowerment revolutionised the women's movement in India providing it unprecedented success and propelling women into a position of utmost importance. The proof of this importance is the 73rd Amendment of the Constitution of India which reserved one Third seats for women in the Panchayati Raj Institutions (PRI) ensuring their participation in the grassroots level. To what extent this initiative met its ends is another issue. However, it certainly suggested a significant change of attitude concerning women in the context of development. There are many other similar examples of this changing attitude towards women in India a primary one of which is application of gender budgeting for ensuring proper budget allocation for development and empowerment of women. Thus, in the words of S.L. Sharma, "the rise of gender sensibility is one of the distinguishing features of our time" (Sharma, 2000).

Now, the question arises, to what extent in reality, women in India has been benefited by this new approach? History tells us that women occupied positions of significance in pre-Vedic periods specifically under the Gupta period which is termed as the 'golden age' in Indian History. Literature in later period indicates a decline in that position of women. Scholars have pointed out various causes behind this decline. A very important one is the patriarchal structure of Indian society. Due to patriarchal domination, women in India are considered to be trapped in domestic drudgery and remain second class citizens. Family as a social institution ensures the production and reproduction of this inequality between men and women and in turn ensures women's subjugation. Although, with the coming of liberalisation of the economic policies, globalisation, spread of education and other similar factors, the condition of women, indeed, have changed. By no means, however, we are in a position to claim that this change is so significant that it represents the emancipation of women from patriarchal bondage and their true empowerment. How, then we are to assume that the new approach towards women in the context of development has or will be able to bring positive change in regard to women's status in India? And if this new approach is failing to achieve its designated ends; which, unfortunately, many of the contemporary studies suggests being the fact; we have no other choice but to investigate and find out the reasons behind it.

In this context, this chapter has examined individuality in Indian society as a factor that impedes the capability of women to attain the benefits of the development practice and attempts of their empowerment. The concept of individuality in India, as has been attempted to highlight in this chapter, is different than the one in the Western society. In fact, if we examine closely and consider Western individuality, we might as well claim that individuality does not exists in India at all, at least in the manner it exists in the West. Western individuality is based on the basic premise that an individual is free to act upon his/her own will, that he/she has a completely separate and distinguished existence beyond his/her social bonding. The Indian 'individual', however, exists only in relation to the society. This relation between the society and the individual is a relation of duties and sacrifice which alone determines the nature of 'individuality' of the individual. Women, under these circumstances, have less scope of asserting their individuality, considering her already undermined position in Indian society. Hence, this chapter has attempted to examine individuality in India as one of the prime reasons behind women's inability to benefit from the process of development. The chapter borrows Amartya Sen's concept of capability deprivation. Sen, in his phenomenal work, 'Development as Freedom' says that the goal of development should be to ensure and extend the freedoms enabling people to remove the inequalities present in the society. He argues, freedoms are not only the ends of development, but also its primary means (Sen, 2000). Here he understood poverty as not just a problem in itself but as a factor that creates lack of ability to achieve other goals and solve other problems and used the term 'capability deprivation' for it. Borrowing this concept, this chapter argues that the state of individuality in Indian society represents a 'capability deprivation' on the part of women when it comes to development and their empowerment.

Significance and Limitations of the Study

This chapter deals with an issue which is undoubtedly represents one of the most striking features of the socio-economic and political scenario, not only in India but throughout the world, i.e. empowerment of women and development. Women empowerment and their place in the development practice is one of the most researched issues today in the fields of Sociology, Economics and many other disciplines. This issue has drawn the attention of not only the academia but also the state and policy makers. Hence, it can be said with utmost conviction that the issue in hand holds significance. However, this chapter is limited in its scope as it's a theoretical take on the issue based on secondary sources. As a result, this chapter has just been able to focus on individuality as a significant factor and make an argument in its favour. The arguments that this chapter has made will require empirical proof which must be based on in depth qualitative analysis of primary data. However, this chapter certainly provides a strong hypothesis for further enquiry.

Development, Empowerment and Women: The Indian Scenario

As stated earlier, the beginning of a distinct interest on the subject of status of women was marked by Ester Boserup's famous work 'Women's Role in Economic Development' in the early 70s. This study pointed out the 'gender gaps' in the distribution of work, resources and benefits. She observed that women do far more work than men do, yet they have only limited access to economic resources and benefits which are largely appropriated by men (Sharma, 2000). These realisations helped in the initiation of the first steps towards women's development in India, which took the form of Welfare Approach. This approach was to recognise women's problems and taking steps to alleviate their status.

Later, the ineffectiveness of the welfare approach led to the emergence of Women in Development (WID) approach in India. The essence of this approach was a realization that a more gendered approach to development can maximize women's potential to contribute to development. In this context the first variant of WID approach emerged which was the Equity Approach which demanded equality for women in socio-economic and political spheres (Sarker, 2006). Women in Development approach took various other forms such as the Policy Efficiency Approach which recognized that not only women need development, but the need is mutual and proper integration of women in the process of development can benefit women and the development process itself.

Gender and its understanding played a crucial role in the evolution of the approaches towards women and development. The Neo-liberal approach towards women advocated that a free market economy will create opportunities for men and women alike. But this idea was shattered by the unequal gender relations existing in the Indian social structure. Critique of this 'gender-neutral' attitude of Neo-liberalism led to the coming of the second approach towards development which was the Gender and Development approach (GAD) (Sarker, 2006). GAD advocated empowerment of women in order to do away with unequal relations of power between men and women in society.

Thus, various theoretical debates on the issue of gender in relation to development has changed and shaped the way how development sees women and their needs. For example, early development practices focused on women's family related problems and responsibilities as that was considered as the female domain. However, with the evolution of theoretical approach on gender the perspective of development also evolved and led to the emergence of various elementary notions of development such as equity, sustainability, productivity etc. along with various development approaches such as engendering, gender mainstreaming, gender planning, gender budgeting etc.

Engendering or engendering policies of development advocate a conscious and continuous attempt on formulation of laws and schemes which are gender sensitive. In fact engendering emphasizes a 'gender awareness' in everything we do and hence we now have ideas like 'engendering governance'. Gender mainstreaming is distinctive in feature in the sense that it seeks to institutionalize equality by embedding gender sensitive practices and norms in the structures, processes and environment of public policy (Daly, 2005). On the other hand, gender planning and gender budgeting focus on gender sensitive policy making and education in order to ensure equal opportunities for women in society. All these perspectives are based on a conscious recognition of gender and inequalities of gender that are present in society which has been explicitly established within the development discourse by the wide range of theoretical debate over gender as a concept.

Another such approach, steered by the debates over gender inequality is the empowerment approach. Empowerment of women has become the key measure of ensuring gender equality and providing equal opportunities and benefits of development to women in India. Empowerment approach attempts to give women power in socio-economic and political spheres. By empowering women, empowerment approach gives women the power to create opportunities for themselves to be on equal grounds with men in society. Empowerment has many attributes such as ensuring women's participation in decision-making process. However, Jo Rowlands suggests that empowerment does not mean just participation in decision-making process, but also include processes that lead people to perceive themselves as able and entitled to make decisions (Rowlands, 1997).[1]

S.L. Sharma points out that the most important aspect of this approach is that conscientization holds the key to women's empowerment. Conscientization refers to a critical awareness about the structure of discrimination, exploitation and oppression in which one is placed. Sharma also points out two approaches to women's empowerment. The first one is 'sponsored' which refers to the efforts made by the state to improve women's power position by making some statutory provisions and legal enactments. This signifies an approach 'from-above'. The second one is 'self-striven' that refers to empowerment through self-mobilisation and it implies mobilisation 'from-below' (Sharma, 2000).

Andre Beteille, talking about natural inequality suggested that people sometimes appear to be unequally endowed (naturally) because in fact the opportunities available to them are unequal (Beteille, 1983). Hence, in a country like India where women hold much disadvantageous positions in comparison to men, special measures such as the ones discussed in this section are, without any doubt, of utmost importance and necessity.

The Individual, Individuality and Individualism

The concept of individuality is a complex and abstract one which is extremely difficult to comprehend, clearly define and explain. However, any attempt to understand the concept of individuality must begin with the realisation that there are clear distinctions between the concepts of the individual, individuality and individualism.

The individual is a very important category which stands in contrast to collectivity. Hobbes, Locke and Bentham described society as an aggregation of individuals, each striving to maximize self-interest. Such ideas not only bestow the awareness of the individual a distinctive existence, but put in a position ontologically prior to the collectivity (Hinchman, 1990). According to Chas A. Mercier, an individual is a mental construct. For an individual to be constituted it does not necessarily require a separate physical existence. The individual to exist, however, it must be separately contemplatible. Applying this idea, Mercier defines the individual as something "... that which is contemplatible, with respect to its external relations as separate from other things, and with respect to its internal composition as unified" (Mercier, 1918).

The concept of individuality, again, is a highly debated one. Francis Rogers distinguishes between the concepts of personality and individuality. Rogers says that the term personality is derived from the Latin word 'persona' which means mask or the external identity of our which we present to the world and through which we communicate with others. Individuality, on the other hand, is the real I; personality is only the seeming while individuality is the innermost kernel of our being (Rogers, 1921). However, the most important and probably the bitterest debate over the concept of individuality is the one that took place between the liberalists and the communitarians.

The liberalists presented the most radical image of individuality. The liberalists, having their roots in the Enlightenment were preoccupied with the individual and individual rights and argued that the community, tradition, social practices and culture as are not essential for the individual. Such an idea flows from the neo-Kantian theory which suggests that the autonomous self must provide ground for one's ability to exercise one's right to be left alone" (Werhane, 1996). One of the most influential proponents of this idea is Thomas Hobbes. Hobbes argued that human beings, in their natural state, that is, in a state of nature without law, government, culture or societal norms, are not inherently social. Rather, each of us, without constraints, is a distinct individual. Hobbes argues; we enter society not because it is natural or innate to do so, but out of necessity in order to survive, to live in peace, and to satisfy our interests. Hobbes' 'radical individualism' can be summarized in the statement that who we are as social beings derives from who we are as human beings. This gives metaphysical priority to the individual, which is clearly visible in the Western thought which upholds the tradition that individuals have certain fundamental rights just because they are human beings. It is commonly argued that the most basic of these is liberty, at least the liberty to be left alone to do as one pleases and pursue one's own ends (Werhane, 1996).

The communitarians contest this notion of individuality and emphasises the roots of the individual which an individual ought to have in society, community and culture. Every communitarian thinker from Burke and Durkheim to Sandel and MacIntyre; despite of their internal disagreements, argued that the identity of the individual must reflect the historical traditions, practices and narratives that give substance to ideas of virtue and vice, and preserver the self from anomie. MacIntyre even claimed that, in a well-ordered polity, there would not even be a self, an 'I', apart from these traditional patterns. Thus, very simply, individuality can be comprehended as a state where individual human beings are understood as separate, discrete selves aware of themselves as such (Hinchman, 1990).

Lewis P. Hinchman points towards a very important distinction between individuality and individualism. He argues that the view on individuality propagated by the liberalists rhymes more with individualism. Hinchman quoting Tocqueville writes, "Individualism…disposes each member of the community to sever himself from the mass of his fellows, and to draw apart with his family and his friends, so that, after he has thus formed a little circle of his own, he willingly leaves society at large to itself." Thus, individualism denotes a separation of the individual from the society. Individuality, however, differs from individualism and does not imply any isolation of the individual but emphasises its distinctiveness along with its integration with the society and culture (Hinchman, 1990). As Gothe writes, "only mankind combined is the true man, and the individual can only be joyous and happy when he has the courage to feel himself in the whole" (Goethe, 1969). Individualism, thus, denotes a state of individuality where the individual detaches itself from the society and societal obligation and thrives to fulfil its own goals and ends by whatever means it deems to be appropriate. Such a situation can, to some extent at least, be observed, in the Western society which encourages the individual to be free, courageous, and acquisitive and develop keenness to endeavours becoming independent of society and relationships.

Individuality and Individualism in Indian Society

It is not very difficult to realise that the individuality in India is very different from the one that exists in the Western societies. This difference is facilitated by significant differences in terms of traditions, social structure and culture including norms and values and the attitudes and aspirations of the individuals which, to a great extent, are determined by norms and value systems themselves. The concept of individuality is a complex one and only with the adequate knowledge of philosophy and religion one can hope to comprehend this complexity. One must also keep in mind the extraordinary diversity that characterizes India, its landscape, its people, its history, thought, and culture.

Indian philosophy (Hindu Philosophy) projects individuals composed of five sheaths. The four inner sheaths are material which is the body, the senses, the mind and the intellect or the ego. However, only these four material components cannot form the true individual. For making of a complete individual or for an individual to develop a complete sense of his/her individuality; one must have a consciousness of *atman*. The *atman* is a purely spiritual entity (Mascolo *et al.*, 2004).

At the beginning of life, *atman* remains fused together with the other for material components of individuality or self. An individual has to go through a lifelong process in order to become aware of *atman* or become aware of his/her true self. This process of becoming aware of the true self has four primary stages. In the first stage, individuals assume the tasks of studentship (*Brahmacharya*). At this stage the duty of the individual is to acquire knowledge and learn discipline. In the next stage, a person gets married, has children, and assumes the role and responsibilities of householder (*Grihastha*). The third stage is *Vanaprastha* which marks a departure from material possessions. The men stop engaging in economic activities and the women stops taking part in running of the household. In this stage, individuals assume the duties of mentors and take up religious activities. The final stage consists of full renunciation of society (*Sannyasa*). In this stage, the individual renounces worldly concerns and spends his time in contemplation, seeking *moksha* (spiritual emancipation, freedom) (Mascolo *et al.*, 2004). Thus, the Individual in India is a unification of material and the spiritual. Another significant aspect of Individuality in India is that the individual is bound to social relations with the ties of morality (Mascolo *et al.*, 2004).

Miller argues that in contrast to Western societies where the concept of individuality is based on individual rights, in traditional Hindu society the concept of individuality is based on duty (Miller, 1994). In the Western societies, liberal ideal of freedom is the primary factor (Rawls, 1971; Kant, 1989; Kohlberg, 1984). According to this view, an individual is free to do his/her will as long as he/she is not infringing upon the rights and freedom of others; beyond that an individual has no moral obligation towards others. In contrast, in Hindu philcsophy, an individual's duty (*dharma*) makes him/her responsible towards not only family, but also the society (Miller, 1994).

However, the nature of individuality is changing in India. Examining individuality in the backdrop of changing culture and values, Anjali Ghosh argues that although Individuality in India is more collective in nature, it is not limited to that aspect any more. According to Ghosh, the Indian individuality is a mixture of collective and individualistic tendencies (Ghosh, 2012). It is important to note that Anjali Ghosh drew this conclusion based on her study on the values towards achievement among college students (Ghosh, 2012).

Victor S. D'Souza in his study, "Individuation in Indian Society: From Collective Identity to Individual Identity" makes a similar argument. D'Souza states that there is an on-going process of transformation in Indian society from collective identity to individual identity. D'Souza following sociologists such as G.H. Mead argues that societal development and development of individuals occur simultaneously as consciousness of individuality and social structure are interdependent. This interaction between the individual and society, as D'Souza has points out, has initiated a process of 'individuation' in India. He states that, individuation is a process by which individuals in society become differentiated. As a result of this increased differentiation which arises because of the changes in the pattern of society, the concept of individuality shifts from collective to individual identity. He also argues that one of the most important factors behind this process is the changing pattern of role allocation in Indian society. D'Souza also remarks that this process of transformation is similar to the one which transformed the Western society years before India (D'Souza, 2006). D'Souza's study points towards the realities of a changing Indian society. Further, his take on the impact of role allocation upon the state of individuality makes one consider the issue of women and individuality in India. Women, whose roles in Indian society are steadily changing today.

Individuality as 'Capability Deprivation' and Women

The preceding discussion has highlighted two primary issues. The first one is the state of development and empowerment of women in the context of India and the second one is the concept of individuality in the West and in India and the differences between the two. The first one has been analysed from the specific point of view of women. The analysis of the second issue, however, has been gender neutral. But, this gender neutrality does not suggest that there is no difference between men and women when it comes to individuality. As has been discussed in the course of the chapter, the notion of individuality is dependent upon societal norms and values and hence, the cultural and social ethos will demarcate the extent to which a man and a woman are able to assert their individuality.

Now, let us come back to the first issue again. There is no doubt that India as a nation is undergoing tremendous change and that this change has resulted in a realization of the essentiality of women and her contribution for India's present and her future. This realization has resulted in policies (for development of women), strategies (such as gender budgeting and gender mainstreaming for ensuring proper efforts towards betterment of women) and a shift in overall attitude towards women and her potential (represented by the women empowerment initiatives). However, this changing scenario does not necessarily mean that women's condition has change for better. There are many implicit and explicit issues which are still hindering the path of development and empowerment of women. There are a huge number of recent studies which provide testimony to this fact. However, in order to stick with the issue at hand, this chapter has refrained from discussing that part in detail. However, it is indeed safe to say that India still has a long way to go in terms of providing equal share of development to men and women.

One very important reason for this inequality among many is that women are incapable of taking advantage of the development and empowerment initiatives formulated for them. Generally, the reasons for this inability is attributed to the lack of education among women, lack of awareness and the pressure of fulfilling traditional role expectations. These reasons, although valid without question; this chapter argues that one of the primary sources of women's failure to take the benefits of development is their individuality.

This brings us to the second issue. In the discussion on individuality, this chapter has established this fact that individuality in Indian society is different from Western society. Not only in nature but they are also different in their origin, if we consider the fact that Western individuality is based upon individual rights whereas Indian individuality is based upon moral codes of duty. If we will observe carefully, we will see that from the standpoint of cultural ethos, tradition and moral code, it is impossible for individualism (keeping individual goals above social goals) to take hold in Indian society. However, recent studies suggest otherwise. This chapter has shown that the concept of individuality in India is changing and it is moving from collective towards individual identity.

If not a complete shift from collective to the individual; this process of transformation surely suggests a tension between collectivist and individualistic attitudes in India. And this tension can be observed best among women. It is here, Victor S. D'Souza's concept of role allotment affecting the state of individuality becomes relevant. Women in India are undergoing tremendous change. More and more women are getting educated and they are becoming eligible for more and more roles everyday. Taking up new roles changes the self-perception of women and mould their individuality. However, the society is not ready to allow women to acquire these new roles yet. More importantly, women themselves, at many times do not take those roles as many women believe firmly that their duty as an individual lies with some other responsibility examples of which are available in plenty. Thus not availing the benefits of development remains no more a lack of opportunity, but it becomes a choice. Whether that choice is spontaneous or imposed; that is a different matter altogether.

Indian society is still evolving and modernizing. Social structure is still patriarchal and women still have a long way to go before they can taste equality in the true sense of the term. Traditional roles of women are still highly valued and there is huge pressure upon women to conform to and perform these roles. Thus, such a society shapes the sense of duties and responsibilities and consequently the individuality of women in India. Even if we accept the view that individuality in India is undergoing a process of change and there is a tension between collective and individualistic attitudes; for those women who are leaning towards individualistic attitudes, letting the opportunities go provided by development and empowerment will be a choice, but not spontaneous. However, if a woman lets go of such an opportunity willingly thinking of her obligation as an individual there may be two reasons behind it. First, she might firmly believe in her roles and duties. Secondly, she will do so out of fear that if she did so she will be considered too individualistic and be accused of ignoring her duties as an individual. In both cases, however, the sense of individuality stands as a barrier for women in terms of availing the benefits of development. The concept of empowerment states that for a woman to be truly empowered, she must have decision making abilities, among other things. Now, even if a woman has that ability, will she be able to make decisions in her own favour ignoring her children, her husband and other family members? A woman who grew up imbibing the traditional value based individuality most certainly will not be. Hence, with conviction, this chapter argues that individuality in India is a major factor of 'capability deprivation' for women in the context of development in India.

Concluding Remarks

This chapter is a very crude attempt of a qualitative analysis of individuality acting as a barrier for women denying them the ability to be advantaged from the developmental policies in India. Through meticulous analysis of relevant secondary sources this chapter has argued that individuality in India emphasizes duties of individuals and sacrifice in performing these duties. Such views are imposed even more strictly when it comes to women. Thus, women's sense of individuality refrain her from diverting from her allocated duties and disables her in terms of taking the advantage of developmental policies. This disability, whether spontaneous, self-imposed or forced by the fear of acquisition of 'individualism'; represents a 'capability deprivation' for women in India. However, here certain very sensitive questions come to fore. If following moral codes and standards of individuality prescribe to women by the society makes women unable to take advantage of developmental policies should they simply abandon those codes and standards? Should Indian women simply abandon their individuality guided by sense of duty and sacrifice and choose 'individualism'? If not, what strategies should be adopted for making women capable of taking advantage of development? Or is there a requirement of re-thinking of the definitions of development and empowerment in the specific context of women in India? These questions most certainly open up areas for further qualitative and in-depth sociological enquiries.

NOTE

1. The concepts of engendering, gender mainstreaming, gender planning, gender budgeting and empowerment that has been discussed in this chapter are multidimensional. There are ambiguities present in these concepts regarding their actual usefulness and applicability in fulfilling the objectives they uphold. There has been a lot of theoretical debate over such issues and much more considerations are still needed in terms of the potential of these concepts in specific situations of gender discrimination, gender relations and development needs in various social setup. However, due to constraint of space, these debates have been left out of discussion in this chatper. For further details please refer to Weiringa (1994), Rowlands (1997), Rowlands (2006), Daly (2005) etc.

REFERENCES

Beteille, A. (1983). *The Idea of Natural Inequality and other Essays.* New Delhi: Oxford University Press.

Boserup, E. (1970). *Women's Role in Economic Development.* New York: St. Martin's Press.

Daly, M.E. (2005). *Gender Mainstreaming in Theory and Practice.* Social politics: International Studies in Gender, State and Society. Vol. 2. No. 3. pp. 433-450. Oxford University Press.

D'Souza, Victor S. (2006). Individuation in Indian Society: From Collective Identity to Individual Identity. *Sociological Bulletin,* Vol. 55, No. 2 (May-August 2006), pp. 281-299. Indian Sociological Society. URL: http://www.jstor.org/stable/23620556. Accessed: 09-09-2015 08:35 UTC.

Ghosh, A. (2012). Individualist-Collectivist Orientations and Achievement Value in College Students. *Journal of Transpersonal Research,* 2012, Vol. 4 (1), 39-46. ISSN: 1989-6077. URL: http://www.transpersonal journal.com/pdf/vol4-issue1/Anjali%20Ghosh.pdf. Accessed: 02:53 PM 25-08-2015.

Gothe, Johann Wolfgang von (1969). *The Autobiography of Johann Wolfgang von Gothe.* Tomes I and II. New York: Horizon.

Hinchman, Lewis P. (1990). The Idea of Individuality: Origins, Meaning, and Political Significance. *The Journal of Politics,* Vol. 52, No. 3 (Aug., 1990), pp. 759-781. Published by: on behalf of The University of Chicago Press Southern Political Science Association. URL: http://www.jstor.org/stable/2131826. Accessed: 09-09-2015 08:31 UTC.

Kant, I. (1989). *The Foundations of the Metaphysics of Morals*. Upper Saddle River, N.J.: Prentice Hall. (Originally published 1785)

Kohlberg, L. (1984). *The Philosophy of Moral Development: Moral Stages and the Idea of Justice*. New York: Harper Collins.

Mascolo, M.F., G. Misra and C. Rapisardi (2004). *Individual and Relational Conceptions of Self in India and the United States*. URL: https://www.academia.edu/211965/Individual_and_Relational_Conceptions_of_Self_in_India_and_the_US. Accessed: 02:40 PM 25-08-2015.

Mercier, Chas. A. (1918). *Individuality*. Mind, Vol. 27, No. 105 (January, 1918), pp. 22-39. Published by Oxford University Press on behalf of Mind Association. URL: http://www. jstor.org/stable/2248823. Accessed: 09-09-2015 08:30 UTC.

Miller, J. (1994). *Cultural Diversity in the Morality of Caring: Individuality-Oriented Versus Duty-based Interpersonal Moral Codes*. Cross Cultural Research. 1994. 28(1). pp. 3-39.

Rawls, J. (1971). *A Theory of Justice*. Cambridge, Mass.: Harvard University Press.

Rogers, Francis (1921). Personality and Individuality. *The North American Review*, Vol. 214, No. 791 (October, 1921), pp. 514-517. University of Northern Iowa. URL: http://www.jstor.org /stable/ 25120852. Accessed: 09-09-2015 08:47 UTC.

Rowlands, J. (1997). *Questioning Empowerment: Working with Women in Homduras*. London: Oxfam.

Rowlands, J. (2006). *Empowerment Examined*. Development with Women (Development in Practice Reader Series). New Delhi: Rawat Publication.

Sarker, D. (2006). Development Theory and Gendered Approach to Development: A Review in the Third World Perspective. In *Sociological Bulletin* (January-April 2006). Vol. 55. No. 1. pp. 45-66. New Delhi: Indian Sociological Society.

Sen, A. (2000). *Development as Freedom*. New Delhi: Oxford University Press.

Sharma, S.L. (2000). Empowerment without Antagonism: A Case for Reformulation of Women's Empowerment Approach. *Sociological Bulletin*, Vol. 49, No. 1 (March 2000), pp. 19-39. Indian Sociological Society. URL: http://www.jstor.org/stable/23619887. Accessed: 09-09-2015 08:26 PM.

Weiringa, S. (1994). Women Interests and Empowerment: Gender Planning Reconsidered. In Doornbos, M.; A. Saith & B. White. (eds.). *Development and Change*. Vol. 25. No. 4. pp. 829-848.

Werhane, Patricia H. (1996). *Community and Individuality*. *New Literary History*, Vol. 27, No. 1, A Symposium on "Living Alone Together" (Winter, 1996), pp. 15-24. The Johns Hopkins University Press. URL: http://www.jstor.org/stable/20057330. Accessed: 09-09-2015 08:31 UTC.

5

Women as Witches, Witches as Homo Sacer, Women as Homo Sacer?

Obja Borah Hazarika

Witch hunting has been prevalent in varying degrees in serveral places of the world throughout history in diverse forms. Although outlawed by law in most countries, witch hunting continues without much ability on the part of the law, the state, and the educated to alter and prevent the practice. In many parts of India witch hunting continues to be reported. States like Assam report witch hunting incidents almost on a daily basis. Despite advocacy against superstitious beliefs which are mainly (but mostly mistakenly) believed to underlie witch hunting incidents, such violation of rights of such people who are victimized as witches, who mostly happen to be female, continue unabated. Continuance of witch hunting thus is a stark reminder of the level of pernicious practices which continue to mar society. It is also a marker of the abysmal level of education and awareness prevailing in several parts of the country. The appalling level of human rights protection available to the victims can also be gauged through the incessant witch hunting cases.

This chapter attempts to pursue a theoretical analysis of the phenomena from the perspective of the concept of Homo Sacer provided by Giorgio Agamben. The study will be conducted with an objective to examine how 'Witch hunting' produces 'witches' as 'Homo Sacer' in today's society which in turn leads to a situation where the victims are devoid of human rights, legal rights or any other rights which are deemed basic or fundamental for living in a meaningful and fruitful way. The societal, cultural, religious, and economic reasons which underlie the creation of the 'witch' as 'Homo Sacer' will be explored in order to provide a theoretical understanding to the phenomena of creating 'women' as 'witches', which in turn leads to 'witches' being situated beyond the reach of law which in turn makes them 'homo sacer', and how that may imply that 'women' are 'homo sacer' in such societies. This chapter thus is grounded in a post-modernist framework provided by Agamben.

Introduction

There are several attributes given to witchcraft in human history, for instance witchcraft has historically been employed to bring about "...the death of some obnoxious person, or to awaken the passion of love in those who are the objects of desire, or to call up the dead, or to bring calamity or impotence upon enemies, rivals and fancied oppressors"(Begum, 2010). Ronald Hutton has identified five characteristics generally shared by those who believe in witches and witchcraft across different cultures and time periods: "(a) witches use non-physical means to cause misfortune or injury to others; (b) harm is usually caused to neighbours or kin rather than strangers; (c) strong social disapproval follows, in part because of the element of secrecy and in part because their motives are not wealth or prestige but malice and spite; (d) witches work within long-standing traditions, rather than in one-time only contexts; and (e) other humans can resist witches through persuasion, non-physical means (counter magic), or deterrence including through corporal punishment, exile, fines or execution" (Hutton, 2004).

Along with the existence of a belief in witchcraft there has also existed witch hunting in human history, prevalent over many countries throughout the ages. Witch hunting implies killing or hurting of the so-called 'witch' mostly by community members. There are reports of various treatments m ted out to witches by the attackers; most of these aims to cause injury and hurt. Mostly "...helpless 'witches' are hounded and punished by being stripped naked, paraded around the villages, their hair is burnt off or their heads tonsured, their faces blackened, their noses cut off, their teeth pulled out (they are supposedly defanged) so that they can no longer curse, they are whipped, they are branded, sometimes, they are forced to eat human excreta and finally, they are put to death (the victim is hanged, impaled, hacked, lynched or buried alive)" (Singh, n.d.). Where these women are left to live, they are considered "...inauspicious and malevolent, socially ostracized and forced to forego their livelihood. Where they don't end up losing their life, they are made to lose their mental balance" (Singh n.d.). Sometimes, if the witch is not killed the family will be socially confined and will be boycotted by the whole village and the community. This will result in loss of livelihood and movement will be restricted. This may also cause in forced migration or displacement and may cause illegal trafficking too (Begum, 2010).

The killing of accused witches continues to be reported from countries like Indonesia, Sri Lanka, India, Barundi, Uganda, Cambodia, Papua New Guinea, Ghana, United Republic of Tanzania, South Africa, Angola, Mali, Democratic Republic of the Congo, Nigeria, Nepal etc. (Begum, 2010). Earlier it was prevalent in Europe and America as well. Until the thirteenth century, the belief that there was such a thing as a witch was considered by church officials to be superstitious nonsense (Nelson, 1975). However, witch hunting became a norm in the following centuries. During the period from 1400 to 1700, an estimated 500,000 to 1 million people were burned as witches in Europe (Ruether, 1975).

In Reformation Europe it was overwhelmingly women who were tried as witches. In 1484 Pope Innocent VIII issued a bill making witchcraft a form of heresy and empowering inquisitors to eradicate this cancer from Christendom. The Malleus Maleficarum (The Witches' Hammer) by Jakob Sprenger and Henry Kramer became a classic statement of misogynism as it articulated the reasons why women were witches. The authors claimed that the term female came from the word femina, which meant "lacking in faith". The basic premise of the Malleus was that witches are pawns of the devil and that the devil recruits his agents through carnal lust. As they put it in the Malleus, "All witchcraft comes from carnal lust, which in women is insatiable." In fact, the inquisitors taught that witches ride broomsticks at night to "black Masses" in which they fornicate with the devil and feast on roasted children (Nelson, 1975).

Witch Hunting in India

Witch hunting is practiced in some form or the other in different parts of India, but mostly concentrated in the areas (states/UTs) of Andhra Pradesh, Assam, Bihar, Chhattisgarh, Gujarat, Jharkhand, Karnataka, Madhya Pradesh, Maharashtra, Orissa, Rajasthan and West Bengal. Mostly, "...middle aged and elderly single women in tribal as well as non-tribal communities are orchestrated as witches, leading to social stigma, displacement, economic boycott, torture and even murder (Chakrabarty and Borah, 2013)." Even men are sometimes labelled as witches.

According to the National Crime Record Bureau between 2008 and 2012, more than 768 women have been murdered for allegedly practicing witch craft. The rate of conviction in cases of crime against women is the lowest in India (26.9%) when compared to other crimes and adding to this crisis is the fact that there is no specific law in India to fight against witch hunting. Witch hunting cases are currently registered under sections 302 (murder), 320 (grievous hurt), 351 (assault), 354 (assault or criminal force to woman with intent to outrage her modesty), 364a (kidnapping for ransom) and 503 (criminal intimidation) (Chakrabarty and Borah, 2013). There are three states in India which have laws against witch hunting: Bihar was first state in India to pass the Prevention of Witch (*Dayan*) Practices Act of 1999. This was followed by Jharkhand's Anti-Witchcraft Act in 2001 along with the 2005/2006 Chhattisgarh and Rajasthan laws. The Assam Assembly in August 2015 unanimously passed the Assam Witch Hunting (Prohibition, Prevention and Protection) Bill, 2015 which rendered offence under the Act as non-compoundable to eliminate the superstition from society as well as non-bailable and cognizable. Project Prahari by Assam Police is another measure to curb this crime. This project, however, is not a continuous action (Begum 2010).

In the north-eastern region of India, which is home to diverse indigenous communities, the practice of witch hunting is prominent. The practice is more prominent, though not limited to, the Rabha, Hajong, Mishing, Bodo and the Adivasi and tea community in Assam (Chakrabarty and Borah, 2013). Witch hunting is still very common in districts of Goalpara, Kokrajhar, Chirang, Baska, Sonitpur, Udalguri, Tinsukia, Dhemaji etc. of Assam. According to available statistics, 81 cases of witch-hunting were reported in the state between 2006 and 2010 (Begum, 2010). The method in identifying and then punishing the 'witch' follows a similar pattern in most of the cases reported. At first instance the "...witch is called a *'daini'* in local parlance and believed to cause ailment to people, destroy crops and other livestock etc. She is usually identified by an *'ojha'*, *'bez'* or *'deodhani'* (all names for witch doctors) and either banished from the community or killed. Sometimes the designated family of the witch is levied a hefty fine by the community leaders, by which she may be pardoned of her ill deeds/intentions against the fellow villagers" (Chakrabarty and Borah, 2013). In addition, the belongings and the properties of the woman is taken away by the people.

Some contend that witch hunting aims to rob the woman of her property. Sometimes it is also directed as punishment for turning down sexual advances or even to settle any grouse that some person with say in village politics might nurse against that woman. Those who seek to rob the woman may be her own family. But in situations where the woman is 'unprotected' (in our patriarchal set-up), i.e. she is a widow or a single woman, there is no shortage of people eyeing her land or other wealth. Witch-hunters (or property-hunters), irrespective of being family members or outsiders, often use the services of *'ojhas'* or 'witch-doctors' to further their cause. In many rural communities with limited or no access to health care, these *ojhas* become powerful figures. Police investigation has found, in many cases, that the local *ojha* has accepted a bribe to name a woman as a witch (Singh n.d.). A witchcraft accusation can be the result of a land conflict or of economic rivalries and competitions, or it can mask the refusal to support family or community members that are seen as a drain on its resources, or can be a devise to justify the enclosures of communal lands (Federici, 2008).

There is another reason which has been forwarded to explain resurgence of witch hunting in Africa which can be applied to India and Assam's witch hunts in particular. In this view, argued by most contemporary anthropological studies, it is stated that witch-hunts are not a legacy of the past, but are a response to the social crisis that globalization and neo-liberal restructuring of Africa's and Asia's, especially India's political economies have produced. Justus Ogembo in "Contemporary Witch-hunting in Gusii, South-western Kenya" (2006) argues that structural adjustment programmes and trade liberalization have so destabilized African (and Asian) communities, and undermined their reproductive system and thrown households into such "deprivation and despair" which people are not able to comprehend, that many people have come to believe that they are the victims of evil conspiracies, carried out by supernatural means (Ogembo, 2006). He points out that, after Kenya (and in the same fashion, India) "adjusted" its economy, which led to unemployment, currency devaluation, so that basic commodities became unavailable, state-subsidies to basic services, like education, health, public transport, were gutted. In short, millions of people, in rural and urban areas, found themselves unable to provide for their families and communities and without any hope for the future. This led to 'rising mortality rates, especially among children, due to the collapse of the healthcare system, growing malnutrition, and the spread of AIDS, contributed to fuel suspicions of foul play leading to a situation where some were targeted as witches who were the source of all these ill happenings. Ogembo argues that the persecution of witches was further instigated by the proliferation of fundamentalist sects, re-injecting into religion the fear of the devil, and by the appearance of self-defined "traditional healers," exploiting people's inability to pay hospital fees and hiding their incompetence behind appeals to the supernatural (Ogembo, 2006).

Agamben and Witch Hunting in Assam and Elsewhere

This chapter attempts to understand the modern day phenomena of witch hunting in Assam and elsewhere as the continuance of 'homo sacer', 'bare life', 'biopower' and 'state of exception' as used by Agamben to describe life in Western democracies or in concentration camps where the sovereign or the government has control not only over the territory but over the bodies of the people as well. The term "...homo sacer itself once referred, in ancient Rome, to a person excommunicated from society, removed from the safeguards offered to its normal members so that his biological life subsequently could be taken by anyone with impunity" (Fiskesjo, 2012).

The state of exception in ancient Rome was created when "...normal political rights and legal safeguards were stripped away, so that the homo sacer was reduced to the mere naked, or bare, life of a human being alive only in a biological but not in any political sense, since he has none of the usual rights of a member of society" (Fiskesjo, 2012). Agamben, however, says that such conditions exist today, when citizens of democratic or modern day governments also lose control of their own bodies, manifested in biometric deposits or concentration camps depending on the intensity of government control. Thus, no one is free, everyone is at risk of becoming homo sacer at the will of the government. Even those with safe citizenship status can at any moment become homo sacer, for example, under Emergency Law between 1975-77 in India, when fundamental liberties were suspended and right to political life was taken away in one swipe.

Agamben[1] insists that democratic states of the West are built on the mechanism that produced homo sacer, and are not fundamentally different from that which enabled Hitler's concentration camps. Agamben insists that for "...those safely holding membership in present-day Western societies, how the built-in threat of their own exclusion from its protections and their acquiescence in this order of things (such as the acceptance of government and corpocratic surveillance; the black prisons and Guantánamo as a permanent state of exception) is the foundational mechanism of power in these modern states" (Fiskesjo, 2012).

Agamben's device of using Ancient Roman law of Homo Sacer and Foucault's concept of state's control over peoples bodies, bio power, to explain today's State's control over the population, helps one examine the phenomena of witch hunting in Assam and elsewhere.

For the accused witch, banishment marks an entry into a state of exception—which is a concept in the legal theory of Carl Schmitt, which indicates a situation which is similar to a state of emergency, but based in the sovereign's ability to transcend the rule of law in the name of the public good. Following banishment the witch becomes reduced to bare life and violent closures to witchcraft related insecurities become legitimate, in a fashion similar to what happened to Homo Sacer in ancient Rome and to the inmates in the concentration camps and to those in Abu Gharib—who are outside the law and can be killed without the killer being accountable for the act, thereby stripping them of any rights whatsoever and depositing them in a state of exception. The state of exception is a space devoid of law. When community chiefs and family elders or *ojha's* or beg's expel the witch from the community, they suspend the general norm of community orientation, very akin to what the sovereign does to inmates in the concentration camps or what Hitler did to Jews.

Under normal circumstances a person belongs to both the community and the family. Membership in a village means that one is entitles to social, cultural, religious, community support and help and protection. However, on being proved a witch, when the witch is banished, she no longer enjoys this protection. The witch instead becomes a security challenge for the village from whom the villagers need to be find protection and thus she is reduced to being a homo sacer and banned—or made to go into the state of exception. She becomes excluded from the moral community in a very physical manner and deprived of her human rights by being banished from the village and the protection thus far given to her is lifted. In this condition, everybody might legitimately expose her to violence thus challenging her material security, and the integrity of her body. She might be tortured and subjected to other human rights abuses. Because the witch is a dangerous person it becomes both legitimate and necessary to eliminate her, either physically by killing her or geographically by driving her away from her home town.

Because of the dangerousness of the witch, she becomes stripped of her rights and reduced to bare life. This implies that labelling somebody a witch legitimises a politicisation of human life, a biopoliticisation of the body of the witch. When a chief or a family elder decides upon banishment of the witch, they draw an outer limit of the moral community and make a distinction between valuable and non-valuable life. In other words the moral community comes into being by excluding somebody and thereby creating the boundaries of the community. The one who is banned is abandoned by law, exposed and threatened. Her life can only be lived on the mercy of others and the others can kill her without regret or accountability. Being cast out of the community means that her life is meaningless. When the witch is banished she goes from being in a position of qualified life to bare life. The banished witch is thus a figure akin to Agamben's homo sacer. The cases of violence analysed below indicate that, like homo sacer, the witch occupies a zone of indistinction between life and death, human and animal. Through banishment the witch becomes bereft of her bios. The witch can be treated in an inhuman and degrading manner because she is not regarded as human. She can be "hounded and punished by being stripped naked, paraded around the villages, their hair is burnt off or their heads tonsured, their faces blackened, their noses cut off, their teeth pulled out (they are supposedly defanged) so that they can no longer curse, they are whipped, they are branded, sometimes, they are forced to eat human excreta and finally, they are put to death (the victim is hanged, impaled, hacked, lynched or buried alive) without any accountability to law" (Singh n.d.). Additionally, everybody might subject the witch to violence. According to Agamben, the one who is banned is somebody who may be considered as dead and whom everybody may legitimately harm. Through expulsion from the village community the witch suffers social death. Homo sacer is thus somebody towards whom everybody can act as sovereigns, not just the government. Everybody might decide the fate of the witch/homo sacer. It is a figure that might be killed with moral impunity. After banishment, the imposition of the state of exception with regards to the witch, authorities and commoners become entangled. Every member of the community might begin to act as sovereigns towards the witch, performing violent acts that further constitute the accused witch as the embodiment of the existential threat of spiritual attacks. The witch falls victim to community's violence.

Conclusions

Although, the witch hunts of today seem to fall into the 'homo sacer' category provided and used by Agamben, it is noteworthy to mention that in Agamben's analysis he only laments the doings of the state or a leader like Hitler as policing the bodies of his people, but in the witch hunting cases, it is the locals who can act as the sovereigns even before the witch becomes as witch, in witch hunting, the locals are the sovereigns who decide on the fate of the witch, making her homo sacer. In this same light, it can also be argued that dowry deaths, dowry persecution and some other evils in which a person is rendered without political life and is ill treated even by their own family is rendered as a homo sacer by the family which in turn becomes the sovereign. In all these cases, it signals a miserable lack of natural justice or human rights prevalent in today's society.

It is also to be noted that since most witches since antiquity have been women. Women's rights and bodily control has been the topic of many debates, both political and academic. From merely fighting for women's socio-political rights, the debate has been enlarged to include the control of women over her body. As shown earlier, one of the causes underlying witch hunting is the fact that women are seen as a burden, as a contender for family property, strong willed women are seen as a threat to patriarchal norms and some have even opined that women whose skills as midwife's and knowledge of herbs was seen as a threat to men's domination and with a view to prevent such independence among women, the witch theory was used to nip such developments. History is replete with torturous treatments meted out to women in the form of *Sati*, female genitalia mutilation all on the basis of some ill-conceived socio-religious-cultural-economic viewpoints. Witch hunting, though admittedly not confined to women, is another such drudgery faced by women. Since, it has been established earlier in the essay that witches are homo sacer, and now it is seen that witches are mostly women, it is safe to opine that in such circumstances women are homo sacer (at least more than the men) in places like Assam (where 77 people were killed and 60 injured in witch-hunt attacks in the state between 2010 and February 2015) and wherever else witch hunting or any such practices prevail where the community or common man becomes the sovereign with the power of destroying another's life by declaring that she is a witch and thereby strip her off her village security, protection and community life and expose her to life as a non-entity who can be killed without accountability on part of the killer (Santoshini, 2015).

The practice of witch-hunting constitutes an extreme form of violence against women, which continues in places like Assam. The State at the Central level as well as the regional level should adopt appropriate measures to eliminate the practice of witch hunting, prosecute and punish those involved, and provide for rehabilitation of, and compensation to, victimized women. Creating public awareness of forms of violence against women rooted in custom as an infringement of women's human rights should be taken up by NGOs and the State as well. Organizations like Assam Mahila Samata Society, All India Democratic Women's Association, Assam Chah Mazdoor Sangha, All Bodo Women Justice Forum Assam Network etc have been trying to stamp out this evil practice but more effort is required given the continuance of the banal practice. Though accused women can take help from the legal system, they are unable to do so because of their displacement, loss of livelihood, lack of community and family support. It is still regarded as a social rather than a criminal issue. Proper education, health facilities, economic opportunities especially in rural/remote areas, will enable the issue to be tackled. If the argument about the family or the village as the new sovereigns deciding the fate of hapless women by blaming them as witches is pursued it can be noted that dangerous social collapse is in the offing. It is a manifestation of banal beliefs and practises which are being misused by people for fulfilling their malicious agendas which are mainly mediated by economic motivations, created by the onset of the pernicious impacts of globalisation, growth without development, among other socio-economic tendencies which are spreading into regions in a way more intrusive and powerful than ever before. Human life and rights are being rapidly undone by the fact that not just the state but powerful local personalities, quacks, sorcerers, local thugs are amassing power over other peoples bodies in their own hands and a phenomena of a state of exception within a state of exception is being created.

NOTE

1. See Agamben, Giorgio (1998): *Homo Sacer: Sovereign Power and Bare Life,* CA: Stanford. Foucault, Michel (2008): *The Birth of Biopolitics: Lectures at the Collège de France,* 1978—1979, New York: Palgrave Macmillan.

REFERENCES

Begum, Ara Anjuman (2010). "The Practice of Witch hunting: A Call for its Abolition AMSS Report", Assam Mahila Samata Society (Mahila Samakhya) Assam. URL: http://www.assammahilasamakhya.org/hunting.pdf. (Accessed on 27.04.2016).

Chakraborty, J. and A. Borah (2013). "Witch hunting in Assam: Strategising Alternative Media for Women Empowerment and Overcoming Superstition", *Journal of North East India Studies,* Vol. 3, No. 2, pp. 15-24.

Federici, Silvia (2008). "Witch-Hunting, Globalization, and Feminist Solidarity in Africa Today", *Journal of International Women's Studies*, Vol. 10, No. 1, pp. 21-35.

Fiskesjo, M. (2012). "Outlaws, barbarians, slaves Critical reflections on Agamben's homo sacer," *Journal of Ethnographic Theory*, Vol. 2, No. 1, pp. 161-180.

Hutton, Ronald (2004). "Anthropological and historical approaches to witchcraft: potential for a new collaboration?", *Historical Journal*, Vol. 47, No. 2, pp. 413-434.

Nelson, Mary (1975). "Why Witches Were Women." In Freeman, J (ed.) (1975): *Women: A Feminist Perspective*, Mayfield: Palo Alto.

Ogembo, Justus M. (2006). *Contemporary witch-hunting in Gusii, Southwestern Kenya*, Lewinston: The Edwin Mellen Press.

Ruether, Rosemary Radford (1975). *New Woman, New Earth*, New York: Seabury Press.

Santoshini, S. (2015). Hunting down witches in northeast India, *Al Jazeera*, 3-9-2015. URL: http://www.aljazeera.com/indepth/features/2015/09/hunting-witches-northeast-india-150902092226394.html. (Accessed 26.04.2016).

Singh, K. Rakesh (n.d.): "Witch-Hunting: Alive and Kicking". *Women's Link*, Vol. 17, No. 1.

6

Reel and Real Indian Women

Sheetal J. Tamakuwala

Popular Hindi films and television serials made in Mumbai have been wielding a widespread influence on the Indian masses for last three to four decades. People from all different class and divergent cultural ethos have been frequenting these films with their inarticulate but deep desires and tensions. It is very obvious from the fact that media readily accept the changing structures of the films, TV serials and advertisements moulded by differing social factors over the decades. A very critical study and analysis shows a deep relationship among the reality situation and mechanisms of wish fulfilments containing it. This transforms the macro world into a micro world of escapism. It is strange to understand that what exactly a person wants to escape from. This paper tries to argue that while mainstream films and TV serials (media) are now presenting women as a commercial item, a thing for pleasure and entertainment only. This then tends itself to a patriarchal coding and leaves little space for a feminist engagement. A survey on TV serials and advertisements and films unfolds the fact that myths and legends from time provides avenues for daydreaming in the absence of a conscious identity with the complex social reality.

By and large gender inequality and oppression has been a basic reality of the society which initiated the women's movement in India. Historically, women's movement in India is not a product of modern India as its roots can be traced far back to the colonial period. As we know, women of all ages belonging to different castes and classes participated in the national movement along with men to fight against colonialism. Both reform movement as well as nationalist movement impacted the position of women positively as these struggles initiated the issue of equal status to women. Largely speaking the status of women is normally determined by the factors like class, caste, family, education and age. More often than not women are subjugated in the name of religion and tradition. Society evolves and creates images and stereotypes particularly with regard to women through religion, tradition, customs and beliefs and so on.

It is an established fact that women constitute one half of the population of the world. In spite of this, their social, economic and political status is lower than that of men notwithstanding their economic and social contribution. Though women put their best efforts and give all they can for the welfare of the society and family the society does not recognize the importance and value of her work and contribution. Her labour becomes either invisible or less significant for obvious reasons. Meanwhile media stereotypes compounds the problem of unequal gender relations further by creating the belief in the society that many of the gender stereotypes seen in the media hold true in real life too. Save a few exceptions women are reduced to being mere show pieces or sex objects on the screen which reflects her social status. More than 80 per cent of Indian films and advertisements have a man as the protagonist. More often than not the actress merely dances around the trees and gyrates in rain in Indian cinema.

Problem

Social reality in India like in any other societies is intermeshed with diverse cultures that are reflecting in variant gender relations ranging from patriarchal forms to matriarchy. The portrayal of this complex range of gender subjectivity gives an appearance of media's simultaneous sensitivity as well as bias on gender issues. Thankfully the prevalence of gender discourse has ensured that the impact of gender differentiating structures in terms of atrocities such as '*sati*', rape, female foeticide, denial of access to facilities and resources (credit, health care, property) and poor quality of participation in availed avenues is well reported. But on the other side such coverage is interspersed with images of typed male-female roles, beauty as an empowering product and female honour as the epitome of Indian culture. In the absence of defined and institutionalized policies, procedures and mechanisms gender concerns would be at best fall in the realm of individual attribution of meaning. For, the reporting of a rape case may be perceived to be a woman's due for flouting the code of social conduct, a warning or mobilization for grievance redressal, depending on the audience.

Moreover, the lack of formalized structure allows the media

to selectively appropriate the present gender issues contextually in conjunction with the dominant socio-political norms. Thus gender representation in the media is open to the influence of competing tendencies, be in the market, cultural capital, communalism, electoral politics or women's empowerment articulations. The responsiveness of the media to gender can be captured through indicators of gender diversity, gender portrayal and gender policies. However, a look at the disaggregate data reveal that women as broadcasters and on desk jobs have a higher representation than as correspondents. While *Hindustan Times* has only five female reporters out of 35, the *Indian Express* Chandigarh Edition has only six out of a total of 23. The place of women in genuine journalistic role in Indian language newspaper according to Robin Jeffery was found wanting as their numbers were scant, the jobs few and prejudices against them formidable indeed.

Women's media continue to feature glamorous women although their clothes, poses and expressions are now much bolder than they used to be a couple of decades ago. So are the cover highlights as the content still revolves around the traditional staples of fashion, beauty, cookery and relationships. However, there is far more focus on other fashion accessories today and of course, there are notable differences between various advertisements, with each projecting a character than presumably suits its target audience. Even magazines endorse stereotypes for example despite to its international image and cosmopolitan dimension focuses on sex more than any of the others.

In this context advertising industry has successfully convinced women that there is something wrong with all of them, like for instance either their teeth are not white enough or their hairs is not shiny enough or so and so forth. The major television corporations sell their products by convincing consumers to buy their brand products for overweight, for wrinkles, specific shampoos for glossy hair etc.

In the television industry women are portrayed as dependent and vulnerable sex symbols while portraying men as strong and aggressive protectors. The popular characters of Jessica Simpson from the hit reality show "Newlyweds" and Pamela Anderson Lee from "Baywatch" are two examples of the television industry dictating women and men what they are supposed to look like. The same is the case with regard to homemade soaps in various television channels like "Balika Vadhu" and "Bandini". Popular advertisements like Fair and Lovely prescribes fair skin to win, any competition. Thus, we are warned time and again that it is a perquisite to be sexy, fair and presentable for success in life. These sexist and racist stereotypes are produced and aired on television constantly creating a psychological augur.

Another popular stereotype is housewification of women in media which accentuates the existing internalization of housewification among women. Because, if men see portrayal of women's housewification or commodification in media, they are more likely to associate women with these roles in real life too. In short these stereotypes lead to lower self-esteem in women and less regard for women by men and women. As the adage goes, where there is no respect for women, progress for that nation is uncertain. Several studies reveal that these gender stereotypes impact young minds to view in a fixed lenses resulting in low self-esteem, eating disorders, less productivity and depression

Television in India began with the state-monitored national channel Doordarshan in the mid-1970s. Those were the times when having a TV antenna jutting out of a terrace or balcony of a home was considered a status symbol. But in the course of three four decades television is just about everywhere, from homes to tea to tea stalls, from slums to remote villages. However, with the advent of cable television and multiple channels international, national, and regional television shows have a had a hegemonic impact on the collective psyche of the nation.

The film-maker Mahesh Bhatt elaborates on the penetrating power of television:

> Television is almost impossible to avoid. It bombards and overwhelms. Streams of images from distant lands, shaped by the world's best image makers, pour into our homes. And the simple Indian man suddenly goes from being a big frog in a small pond to a small fish in a vast ocean of images, where he is endlessly entertained...... The audio-visual drug has proved to be efficient as a birth-control method in our billion-plus-and-still counting nation. (Blakely, 12)

Imaging Gender on the Small Screen

Indian television soaps and serials have constructed a virtual myth of the contemporary middle-class, upper-middle class, and business-class Indian families. In these serials the changes that have revolutionized the lives of urban Indians, such as microwave dinners, desktop computers, blackberry, laptops, DVD players, working parents instead of a working father and a homemaker mother, creches, children's schooling, caring for senior citizens, fast food, westernized lifestyles, and sartorial preferences are seldom addressed. Instead, the soaps and serials glamorize the roles of plotting, scheming adult women who are bad, and valorize the roles of silent suffering women who shed more tears than speak because they are good women.

Uma Chakravarti (Bel *et al.*: 295-314) locates a paradigm shift from the earlier TV serials that was about national concerns and issues, spanning the historicity of the colonial experience and the post-colonial, from *Buniyaad to Hum Log* and *Tamas* and even *Malgudi Days* along with the epics *Ramayana* and *Mahabharata.*

In India this is significant with the majority of the population being literate or semiliterate. The division between the educated and the literate is very fearful gulf and that bridge is built by visual images. It can be clearly understood that viewers gaze is always subjective gaze. Each women will have its own subjective to watch and perceive the visual images shown in the TV serials. A feminist will be appalled by TV shows where women weep endlessly, while majority of the viewers will smile and weep as the fortunes of the TV persona in the serials rise and fall.

In the television industry women are portrayed as dependent and vulnerable sex symbols while portraying men as strong and aggressive protectors. the popular characters of Jessica Simpson from the hit reality show "Newly weds" and Pamela Anderson Lee from "Baywatch" are two examples of the television industry dictating women and men what they are supposed to look like. The same is the case with regard to homemade soaps in the various television channels, like Ekta Kapoor's dramatic 'K' series serials. Popular advertisement like Fair and Lovely prescribes fair skin to win, any competition. Thus we are warned time and again that it is a perquisite to be sexy, fair and presented for success in life. These sexist and racist stereotypes are produced and aired on television constantly creating a psychological augur. Another popular stereotype is housewification of women in media which accentuates the existing internalization among women. Because if men see portrayal of women's housewification or comodification in media, they are more likely to associate women with these roles in real life too. In short these stereotypes lead to lower self-esteem in women and less regard for women by men and women. As the adage goes, where there is no respect for women, progress for that nation is uncertain. Several studies reveal that these gender stereotypes impact young minds to view in a fixed lenses resulting in low self-esteem, eating disorders, less productivity and depression.

Along with the mass consumption of these family-centric traditional role playing by women in the 21st century, where educated women, professional women, and independent women were marginalized systematically and the religious, nonprofessional women were fore grounded as representative of Indian culture, the other major TV attraction has been the reality shows. Wedding ceremonies seem to be compulsory content in serials, elaborate in rituals, lavish in decor and the bride, groom, and all invites from relatives are seen sporting expensive clothes and jewellery. These images are reiterated in advertisements on public hoardings and print media, thereby it suggests the closeness among the corporate sectors, marketing strategies, and media involvement in constructing images that will create more interest of the consumers.

Some of the Ekta Kapoor soap operas that kept women glued to the sets were Kahani Ghar Ghar Ki, Kasauti Zindagi Ki, Kalash, and Kyunki Saas Bhi Kabhi Bahu Thi. The last mentioned present day epic-serial ran for over eight years, commencing in 2000 and the last episode on the small screen was on May 7, 2009. Newspapers ran reports about how the good wife Smriti Irani was being approached by political parties to be their brand ambassador, if such a phrase can be borrowed to describe political parties that use film and television celebrities as their members. One more case study of another TV serial that drew a lot of attention and criticism was Balika Vadhu (Girl-Child Bride). The serial did glamorize and romanticize child marriage leading to serious protest to ban the serial.

In Asian countries especially India the propensity to prioritize the traditional women and traditional lifestyles with modern frills such as gadgets and gizmos seems to have become a normative media practice as comparative channel switching can readily prove. Deshpande analyses the overall agenda and ideology of TV serials and Bollywood commercial films clearly by stating the following lines: The plots of Bollywood commercial films and prime time television serials are the same in general. These serials are miniature Hindi films wherein the story emanates from a rich, joint, presumed upper-caste and patriarchal family. The women in the serials derive their existence and social status almost entirely from their family hierarchy following the rules and regulations of patriarchy, is determined by male power (Deshpande, 20).

Objectives of the Study

1. To find out various prevalent gender stereotypes particularly in television serials and advertisements;
2. To find out whether stereotypes hold women back from progress or not;
3. To compare the stereotypes of men towards women and *vice versa;*
4. To find out whether or not media is responsible for the stereotyping of women; and
5. To analyze the social cost of gender stereotypes on young women as well as men and their perceptions.

It needs to be mention that any analysis of women cannot be viewed in isolation but from wider context as both men and women constitute society. Accordingly an attempt is made in the present exercise to examine the issue of gender stereotyping in media from a larger perspective, i.e. men and women in society as a whole.

The above mentioned objectives are investigated through an appropriate method of data collection techniques as regard to primary data. Our unit of study is the Post Graduate and Under Graduate female and male students. We have taken a sample of 300 students in all; out of which 100 (50 males and 50 females) from S.P.B. English Medium College in Surat city, i.e. where the rich and elite students study and 100 (50 male and 50 female) from Surat Zillah Sahkari Spinning Vidya Sankul, Olpad with Gujarati Medium which falls in rural area and 100 (50 males and 50 females) from the PG Departments of the University where all sections, rural, urban, tribal, minority etc. are represented. In this context, we have analyzed two serials, namely, 'Balika Vadhu' in Colors channel and 'Bandini' in Imagine Channel respectively to examine the media impact. We have deliberately chosen urban as well as rural college and university students to understand the media influence on different segments specially as the girls and boys enter college after school and later as they enter the Post Graduate studies from the college as this might help to throw some light on the perception changes as well as confirmation with the overall growth of individual beings in the society at large. We used random probability sampling method to enable the chance of fair representation. The significance as well as complexity of the present study necessitates us to use various other techniques of data collection including personal and group interview methods, participant observation and case study methods. Besides we have also used household census schedule to analyze demographic, social, economic, education and cultural background of the respondents. We have used class, gender, and education as variables in the analysis to understand the gender concerns and the impact of gender stereotyping on the respondent population in general and the young girls in particular.

The secondary data are collected from the sources like the concerned literature—books, journals, reports, documents, census, etc. from the Veer Narmad South Gujarat University Central library, library of the department of Sociology and Centre for Social Studies library respectively. In addition, we have also interviewed the women activists and academics to perceive the problem in depth.

Major Findings

Our data reveals the average monthly income ranging between 10,000 to 30,000—from the respondents of Olpad College and S.P.B. College respectively. This showed a clear picture of the economic status of the respondents which further helped to know the environment, culture, socialization, attitude and co-operation. Majority of the respondents whose monthly income exceeds Rs. 30,000 (21%) are from urban area (SPB College) followed by (32.2%) below Rs. 10,000 from rural area (Olpad College) respectively. The basic criterion of taking income as one of the important variable is to analyze the exposure of the respective classes depending upon their income. We came to know that the respondents belonging to S.P.B. College were more open minded and liberal in attitude as opposed to the Olpad College respondents. Needless to mention that, the probability of higher studies and future development depends on the socio-economic condition of the household.

As regard to channel preference of the respondents, we found a huge difference depending upon the area. For instance 30 (30%) respondents from Olpad College, 24 (24%) from S.P.B. College and 25 (25%) from University VNSGU preferred Colors channel. As Olpad College respondents resided in rural area they preferred more to watch daily soap operas as they found connect between their own culture and custom with the Television Serials. It is revealing to notice from the respondents from the Olpad College that television characters are very familiar and matching to their family members, while S.P.B. College respondents were comparatively less interested in Colors Channel, as they were more interested in reality shows whereas University (VNSGU) includes multi-cultural combination of respondents we had mixed view of perceptions and attitudes.

Gender inequality in education is one of the important aspects of education disparity. It is a fact that literacy and educational level of rural areas are below the national average. Educational backwardness among females in rural areas is a matter of particular concern, specially the dropout rate as only a few are able to become successful individuals. It seems that the development and prosperity of Surat city is not spread evenly. Even though majority of respondents are aware of the need of education they are trapped by their situations and surroundings which ultimately affects the education. Attitude towards education is strongly influenced by cultural norms coupled with traditions.

Regarding preference of programmes by the respondents of rural, urban and urban-rural areas we observed that the frequency of respondents watching Balika Vadhu, Bandini, Yeh Rishta Kya Kehlata Hain is 36, 19, 24 is far more as compared to S.P.B. respondents, i.e. 25, 16, 8 respectively. By and large the serials have a similar story line portraying upper class and upper caste, Hindu, Rajasthan Marwadi family. Respondents of the rural areas preferred Balika Vadhu and Bandini sort of serials because of the conservativeness, traditional and feudal mindsets as they tried to associate themselves with the female characters with the qualities of submissiveness, responsibility of domestic chores, control of women sexuality and fertility etc. In addition the female respondents were more interested and attracted by the T.V. serials specially women's dress code, hairstyle patterns, jewellery and above all make up. If we come to the ground reality we hardly find any female wearing saree with makeup and heavy jewellery working in kitchen. Besides the serials Balika Vadhu and Bandini in our study sample have revealed the storyline underlining the men's dominance and supremacy as even men enjoy watching it as they get ego satisfaction.

In our empirical analysis we tried to understand the frequency of reinforcement of gender stereotypes which is reflected from the Television Serials. Majority of the respondents did not believe that the prevalent stereotypes are generated from the Television Serials. We analyzed this perception area-wise and we found that women were more in number than men who did not believe that the reinforcement of gender stereotypes is created or initiated by media through Television serials and advertisements. In our sample 35 (70%) men and 47 (94%) women from S.P.B. College disagreed with the statement (reinforcement of gender stereotypes). Whereas only 15 (30%) men and three (6%) women were in favour. Thus it is not a surprise that 39 (78%) men and 40 (80%) women from Olpad College were not in favour of the assumption while 11 (22%) men and 10 (20%) women agreed with it. Similarly 40 (80%) men and 31 (62%) women from the University (VNSGU) disagreed with the assumption of gender reinforcement, while 10 (20%) men and 19 (38%) women agreed.

The patriarchal mindset subordinates women from birth till their entire life cycle is internalized by women as well as men equally. This process begins from the earliest childhood through socialization process and then reinforced through the cultural, social, and economic arrangements in the society. Women in our study sample serials do not enjoy equal status and do not have decision making powers. The family upholds the gender contract based on limiting women's decision making as their husband in-laws and other elders do not allow the women's participation while patriarchy is emphasized and reinforced in the two Television serials which brain washes the viewers eventually. The families in the serials follow strict rules and regulations where incision, importance of family's pride and honour, rights and rituals are given prime focus. This gives a clear picture of patrilocal and patrilinial system existing in the daily soap operas. Even though women are projected bold they accept the patriarchal value system and also projected as willingly the dominance of male supremacy. Most of the women in all the categories in our study revealed the family and social disapproval of women's decision making and conservative patriarchal attitudes on the one hand and on the other subtle resistance and struggle towards change within the family structure.

We noted that the polarities of male and female behaviour are largely shown as aggressive and confident, while women as shy and responsive in the two serials under study. Women are shown worshipping their husbands, being dependent on them and competent with each other for male favours. Analysis showed that both in fiction and commercials there is a sharp polarization of roles along gender lines. Beauty soaps, toilet soaps, and fairness cream commercials feature glamorous light skin women depicting them as desirable princess. Advertisements for energy drinks and health products feature mothers serving the young sons dreaming in their glory of their bright and prosperous future achievements. By and large in commercials, films and advertisements women are depicted as homebound serving men and children seeking male approval, whereas men are depicted outside home. In case of male characters the range of occupations presented is very wide. They are industrialists, bureaucrats, businessmen, journalists, executives, police officers etc. Advertising agencies reap huge profits by making sexist advertisements featuring women. This form of advertising has become an important tool of perpetuation of male supremacy, which exploits women's sexuality and their physical appearance. The effect is also highlighted by showing equally men and women sharing recreational activities but not work. On the contrary, women are relatively shown with less working roles. Our prime effort through this study is to reveal the fact that how women are being portrayed in media specially advertisements and T.V. serials. Media always depicts women in two major roles, i.e. prime caretakers of the family and sex symbols. During our fieldwork we came to know that not only men but also women have accepted the fact that the prime responsibility of the children, husband, in-laws, house and family totally falls on women. The growing acceptance of the idea that men should also share the task of housework is absent despite globalization and technological changes. This social perception certainly reveals the status of women as well as the perpetuation of gender subordination in family notwithstanding the technological shifts.

It is predominantly believed that television is a window to the world by a majority of respondents in our study. It is also perceived as a medium that gives information and brings awareness in the viewers. The second impact is the influence of television as a source of entertainment and information. Because of poverty and unequal distribution of the social work the poor class is satisfied with TV as a source of entertainment from the long hours of both physical and mental work besides exertion and hence uses this medium as a temporary reliever through films, songs, serials etc.

Our respondents who are college students also agreed to the fact that TV has negative and positive effects on the society. TV affects the culture and children negatively. The respondents revealed that they viewed TV only as a medium of entertainment 225 (99.6%), window to world 120 (97.5%), relaxation and relieving stress 105 (97.2%) respectively. Effects like increasing belief in super natural and fantasy with a negative effect on children (87%-96.5%) and reducing interest in reading and making adults and children inactive, 73 (98.6%) are clear-cut findings from the study. During the interaction with the respondents during our fieldwork we came to know the negative effects diverting from the real issues thus resulting in less socialization, reducing interaction amongst the family members and so on. The impact of television is largely adverse especially on children. Children are initiated to violence by the electronic medium. Television is reported to encourage and influence early sexual activity, drug and alcohol abuse. Our data reveal that as much as 94 per cent respondents watch advertisements on television while six per cent do not. But we were told by our respondents that those who watch advertisements are not really interested but they do not have any choice as they are forced to do so, as advertisements are flicking in between serials. Needless to mention that the children learn without much effort at early age what took many years for their parents to learn.

Television advertisements successfully reinforce the consumerism on the respondents. Market economy has harnessed the medium between the producers and consumers. It is a fact that Advertising on television is used to maintain the economic system which creates a demand among consumers for excellent services, status, life style and other fashionable items and commodities. Thus we found that students across all economic categories hold that patriarchal value system is packaged in advertisements. Not surprisingly the respondents from urban area are more aware of patriarchal implications and consumerism portrayed through television advertisements than the rural areas. The respondents from the rural area are the least aware and the University (VNSGU) respondents fall between the two. Thus the urban college, i.e. S.P.B. English Medium College stands out as the most aware group on gender perception and consumerism and advertisements. This is so not only due to higher educational level but also better economic condition that results in higher degree of awareness.

In our empirical analysis we tried to understand the level of awareness to know the attitude and perception of women about their status and its larger impact on women. With regard to the perception and awareness women across all economic categories justify patriarchal value system. However, gender inequalities in our study serials, namely Balika Vadhu and Bandini are related to themselves more by respondents of the rural area (Olpad College) as compared to urban area respondents (S.P.B. College) and University (VNSGU). This clear difference across classes in the perception of gender inequality as reflected in Television serials also reveals the level of involvement and internalization of the unequal value system more by the Olpad College students. More than 90 per cent of the respondents from S.P.B. College and VNSGU University believe that women should fight against the injustice and similarly a large group believed that career is important for a woman to lead an independent life. Awareness of economic independence was also expressed by Olpad College students but they had to face a lot of personal and family problems in this connection. This is so due to lack of education and ignorance parents did not allow specially girls to study more and earn to be independent. Our study shows that S.P.B. College and VNSGU students are more career oriented and are aware of gender equality. The girl respondents from the Olpad College (rural) feel more of the need for women to fight for justice as portrayed in Television serials while those from S.P.B. College and VNSGU students the priorities are earning money, achieving success through education and to be independent in their lives.

In our empirical analysis we tried to evaluate the level of perception of women on patriarchy and its implications on women through Television serials and advertisements. We look patriarchy broadly as the economic and sexual control of women by men. Patriarchy reinforces the gender division of labour and control of their fertility and their sexuality through the institution of society called "marriage". The data show that female respondents across economic categories legitimizes patriarchal value system and do not raise their voices. However, the researcher was glad to know that the new generation is becoming aware more of themselves and social implications and thus agrees with patriarchal values only to some extent but not like their parents. Meanwhile male respondents have denied about the existence of gender difference as they argue that today women's presence is felt in all professions.

Final Outcomes from the Study

Though in Indian cinema or TV serials women form the central discourse and enact major roles within the familial space, the remote control of their traditional lifestyles and their complex experiences seem to be entirely in the hands of the male members of families. Sometimes this domination is shared with an equally dominant mother or more often mother-in-law who corroborates and consolidates patriarchal norms with a crusader's passion.

Generally, these women are of two kinds. The first display a subdued sexually, are simultaneously docile, obedient, devoted to home making, traditional in the sense of observing rituals like *Karva Chauth*, etc., and carriers of *sanskara* and *parampara*. This second kind is selfish, scheming, vamp like, outgoing and a threat to family stability, often dressed in Western clothes—female Viagra, the supreme threat to male sexual superiority.

In the first decade of the 21st century a paradigm shift in the terms of content and gender perspective became very noticeable. Indian soap operas in Hindi and other regional languages harped on the efficacy of the joint family system, intrafamilial complications that were all planned and conspired by the villain women who victimized the idealized suffering women. This idealized women plays multiple roles as avenger of evil, good daughter in law, supporting wife and above all nurturing mother. The Ekta Kapoor's so called 'K' serials hiked women in promoting religious custom and rituals leading to women fasting and valorizing self-denial and passivity as the desirable track to follow in order to ensure inter and intra-familial harmony and domestic peace and prosperity.

TV advertisements about moisturizing lotions where men in Western wear fantasize about desirable women's skin as being as smooth and silky like strawberries and cream are accepted as normative as the patriarchal media consistently floats these images. A recent Boro Plus and Fair and Lovely television advertisements have very fair, seemingly Western men expressing through their body language the exhilaration of touching a smooth skinned woman.

Visual images of parts of the woman's nude body, including the navel are off-set against men clutching themselves in joyful arousal to recount the so called "*mulayam*" or smooth skinned women. When this ethnic word "*mulayam*" is uttered with relish by the man gyrating joyfully, holding the women tight with his hands is intentionally introduced to destroy the distances and bring home the erotic sensation of touching a Boro Plus-softened female body. The new phrases in the media like "*Khelne chahogey*" "a catch me if you can" used in recent advertisements shows a smooth skinned luscious female who challenges a bunch of men by smiling and running using the phrases to attract them. The woman's smooth and slippery body that the men reach out to clutch but cannot is the ultimate sexist provocative playfulness that a skin lotion can effectively stimulate. The advertisement of Maaza drink depicting Katrina Kaif does not wholly go with the theme. The advertisements is totally illogical where an *aam ras* is marketed by showing the half naked body of an actress. Similarly many commodities not used by women only and only used by men than too objectified and targeted on female sensuality and provocative acts....

Such visual images on television watched by both adult and minor family members merely consolidate stereotyping of gendered images.

Reality shows sponsored by music CD companies such as Sa Re Ga Ma and others have made parents enforce vocal music and dancing as compulsory skills to be acquired by their children. The lure of Bollywood and even the lure of Making fast money have made parents of suburban areas painstakingly train their children to sing, dance, and even perform on the stage. The models to follow are also from the Bollywood either singing or dancing field, and hence girls and boys replicate the singing style of Shreya Ghoshal, Lata Mangeshkar, Asha Bhonsle, and dance like Prabhu Deva, Hrithik Roshan, and Sharukh Khan among others. The TRP ratings of such shows makes the media rather harsh and indifferent towards those who are eliminated in each round, the disappointment and distress that are often seen in the faces of parents and their unsuccessful children. This reality shows makes wonder whether the smooth child parent relationship is destroyed by the desire of gain and fame generated by the need to be successful. Reality dance shows have generated great popular interest and competitive programmes such as Dance India Dance have led to even children gyrating like adult movie stars in Bollywood films. This competitive shows are indeed very popular among the middle class suburban sections of society, as success in such shows leads to the dream of being on the path of stardom and achieving celebrity status.

One such reality show advertisement had a hollering Anu Kapoor shout out, Sing and Get Money, The Big Boss, Rakhi ka Swayamwar are fine examples of best TRPs. The UK reality show Big Brother lead Shilpa Shetty once again as an international recognized celebrity as she protested against racist comments made by her co-inmate of Big-Brother. Another American TV boom show Who will Be a Millionaire led to Amitabh Bachchan anchored Kaun Banega Crorepati, that enjoyed viewership and participation throughout the nation followed by aspiring singer Indian Idol that followed US model of the American Idol. All such shows that involve active viewer participation enforce the binaries of achievers, winners and losers in the minds of the consumers often leading to depression and stress.

To rewind the above findings we infer that there exists a strong socio-economic impact of television medium on women and society in all spheres. No wonder television scores the highest point in preference than newspaper, magazines and radio.

Western models have influenced recent advertisement trends of Diamond, Solitaires, Platinum etc. which appears to a special category of feminine consumers. Engagement and wedding rings are not very common in Asian countries, except minority communities of Christians or Anglo-Indians. Thus similarly, advertisers seem very eager to cash in on the trend by composing such advertisements and forcing the public to set the trend.

To sum up, women as targets of advertisers is as old as the advertising industry. There are certain changes to an extent, however, the ups and downs of society, local factors, economy, globalization have brought changes within the general framework of continuity.

The Need Now

The need of the hour is to get rid of the dominant discourse by evolving an alternative discourse anchored in development and empowerment which will go a long way in the project of emancipation of women. In general, women are the most vulnerable section of our society due to its patriarchal nature.

They are not given enough freedom and suffer from poor access to higher education as even the primary level education is not easily accessible to them. The opening of avenues in employment to women and the rise of women in varied professions should be encouraged to create awareness. Instead of portraying women as housewives and sex symbols women should be presented in media in different assertive roles. Media should play a positive role specially electronic medium in contributing to the overall social consciousness. Women's co-operatives, women's training and production centre should be opened for economic activities for all segments of the society particularly women from the underprivileged class.

We hold that women's position in the society needs to be analysed in relation to production and corresponding power structure. Thus, it is essential to take into account the broader implication of development and thus women's question becomes a social question.

REFERENCES

Ali, R., Das, J., Walque, D., Leonard, K.L., Lundberg, M., and D. Peters (2011), "Patterns of Health Care Interactions in Seven Low and Middle-Income Countries," Background Paper for the WDR 2012.

Ashraf, N. (2009), "Spousal Control and Intra-Household Decision Making: An Experimental Study in the Philippines," *American Economic Review,* 99(4): 1245-1277.

Attanasio, O. and K. Kaufmann (2009), "Educational Choices, Subjective Expectations, and Credit Constraints," NBER Working Paper No. 15087.

Babcok, Linda and Sara Laschever (2003), *Women Don't Ask: Negotiations and Gender Divide.* Princeton: Princeton University Press.

Basu, K. (2008), "Hyperbolic Discounting and the Sustainability of Rotational Savings Arrangements," Mimeo, Hunter College.

Belluck, P. (2011), "If You Really, Really Wanted a Girl ..." *The New York Times,* August 20, 2011.

Chattopadhyay, R. and E. Duflo (2004), "Women as Policy-Makers: Evidence from a Randomized Policy Experiment in India," *Econometrica,* 72(5): 1409-1443.

Chiappori, P., Fortin, B., and G. Lacroix (2002), "Marriage Market, Divorce Legislation, and Household Labor Supply," *Journal of Political Economy,* 110(1): 37-72.

Deaton, A. (1989), "Looking for Boy-Girl Discrimination in Household Expenditure Data," *World Bank Economic Review,* 3(1): 1-15.

Deaton, A. (1997), *The Analysis of Household Surveys: A Microeconometric Approach to Development Policy*.

Desai, S. (1994), *Gender Inequalities and Demographic Behavior: India*. New York: The Population Council, Inc.

Devoto, F., Duflo, E., Dupas, P., Pariente, W. and V. Pons (2011), "Happiness on Tap: Piped Water Adoption in Urban Morocco," NBER Working Paper No. 16933.

Duflo, E., Dupas, P., and M. Kremer (2011), "Education, HIV, and Early Fertility: Experimental Evidence from Kenya," MIMEO.

Gneezy, U., Niederle, M., and A. Rustichini (2003), "Performance in Competitive Environments: Gender Differences," *Quarterly Journal of Economics*, 118(3): 1049-1074.

Goldin, C. and L. Katz (2002), "The Power of the Pill: Oral Contraceptives and Women's Career and Marriage Decisions," *Journal of Political Economy*, 110(4): 730-770.

Goldstein, M. and C. Udry (2005), "The Profits of Power: Land Rights and Agricultural Investment in Ghana," MIMEO, Yale University.

Jayachandran, S., Lleras-Muney, A. and K. Smith (2010), "Modern Medicine and the Twentieth Century Decline in Mortality: Evidence on the Impact of Sulfa Drugs," *American Economic Journal: Applied Economics*, 2(2): 118-146.

Karlan, D., and J. Zinman (2011), "Microcredit in Theory and Practice: Using Randomized Credit Scoring for Impact Evaluation," *Science*, 332(6035): 1278-1284.

Karlan, D., and M. Valdivia (2011), "Teaching Entrepreneurship: Impact of Business Training on Microfinance Clients and Institutions," *Review of Economics and Statistics*, 92(2): 510-527.

Lundberg, S.J., Pollak, R.A., and T.J. Wales (1996), "Do Husbands and Wives Pool Their Resources? Evidence from the United Kingdom Child Benefit," *Journal of Human Resources*, 32(4):463:480.

Miller, G. (2008), "Women's Suffrage, Political Responsiveness, and Child Survival in American History," *Quarterly Journal of Economics*, 123(3): 1287-1327.

NH10. Dir. Navdeep Singh. India, 2014. Film

Rose, E. (1999), "Consumption Smoothing and Excess Female Mortality in Rural India," *Review of Economics and Statistics*, 81(1): 41-49.

Thomas, Duncan (1992), "The Distribution of Income and Expenditures within the Household," *Annales d'Economie et de Statistique*, 29: 109-136.

Thomas, D., Frankenburg, E., and D. Contreras (2002), "Distribution of Power within the Household and Child Health," MIMEO, UCLA.

http://www.bollywoodhungama.com/moviemicro/criticreview/id/576459 (Accessed on 12 Sept 2015)

7

Gender Issues in Family Planning

A Case Study

Maitreyee Sharma

Family planning does not mean only the limitation of births but also highlights the importance of adequate spacing between subsequent births. This is essential for better health of the mother and her children. India is one of the pioneer countries to initiate a family planning programme way back in 1952 in the First Five Year Plan and since then various significant changes have been highlighted in many studies done on the impact of family planning on the population growth. Family planning programmes as organized efforts to give contraception services to men and women were one of the major health and social interventions started in second half the twentieth century (Bongaarts *et al.*, 2012). It is pertinent to note here that the directed social change is often found to be erroneous. India is composed of diverse ethnic groups with their own cultural values which direct the level of fertility in the society. Son preference, though reducing, still persists in India which is evident through continuously declining sex-ratio in the country. Since, fertility is believed to be the exclusive domain of women so it is generally thought that fertility control methods must be applied by the women folk only. Therefore, it is the essential as well as immediate need to change men's attitude and behaviour towards women's health, fertility and make them more supportive to women using health care services and sharing child rearing activities (Helzner, 1996). According to 2011 family welfare programmes, two major achievements quite frequently highlighted are: increase in the acceptance of female sterilization fertility rate among the educated women. Many queries can rise up at this point such as why the educated women exclusively show a decreased rate of fertility and why not the illiterate ones? Why female sterilization is preferred more than the male sterilization in certain cultural group/groups. In India, we know that the female literacy rate is just 65.46 per cent (Census, 2011) and the rest are illiterate and are not aware of policies and programmes. Apart from these, the gender issues that lie implicitly embedded in the conjuncture of awareness and actual utilization of family planning measures are rarely studied and taken into account. One of the Objectives of India's Population Policy 2000 is to achieve a stable population by 2045, so, it is highly essential to expose every married Indian couple to various effective family planning measures and to motivate them to use these effectively. In executing these directed aims it is significant to understand the societal norms and values especially of the tribal groups or any other lesser known ethnic group for proper social and demographic change. These gender issues related to family planning are vital at this moment because of three (03) reasons which create a kind of hegemony mental dilemma and impasse in the decision making process of the females:

(a) Increasing awareness on the benefits of family planning among the females in the urban as well as in the rural areas and their easy accessibility,
(b) Due to patriarchal nature of the societies, the females exclusively are unable to take decisions on the utilization and acceptance of these devices though some of them are aware of the measures and the benefits, and
(c) Every cultural group has certain preferred attitudes and values regarding the ideal number of children born as well as the sex composition of the children in the family which sometimes nullify the first point cited above (a) and the females are implicitly compelled to accept the decision of the husband (b).

This chapter describes the current scenario of implicit and explicit gender issues that hinder the practice of family planning and stresses upon the need of incorporating gender equity in the whole process of family planning. The study is made in a scheduled tribe known as Mishing. It is the second most populated scheduled tribe (plains) in Assam (Census 2011). A micro study has been made in a homogenous village known as Kumarbari in the river island of Majuli, Assam. A semi-structured interview schedule was prepared consisting of socio-demographic information of the couple, family size preferences, gender preferences and causes of such preferences, knowledge, attitude and practice of family planning methods, reasons for using or not using family planning methods, sources of information on family planning devices and suggestions for increasing male involvement and use of family planning methods and devices. The information was collected by the author and classified according to the response given by the respondents as some questions were open-ended. Data related to family planning were collected from the ever-married couples of the village.

Results and Discussion

The population pyramid of the Mishings (Fig. 7.1) shows a childhood bulge at the age cohort of 0-4 years, and the women in the marriageable and child-bearing age-cohorts are higher than the other age cohorts. The population pyramid of the Mishings show that though in the last 15 years the growth rate has slowed down but again in the last 5 years show a sudden bump in the age cohort of 0-4 years. Moreover, the population pyramid also indicates an age-sex structure favourable to the women of child-bearing ages from 20-24 years to 35-39 years. The population is found to be of progressive type but it seems that up to last 5 years, the population was at the second phase of demographic transition when the birth rate has declined gradually. The result is a characteristic ace-of-spades form of population pyramid.

The overall sex-ratio of the population is found to be 105.7 (Number of females per 100 males) (Table 7.1). But, interestingly, when age specific sex ratios are analyzed, it is observed that the Mishings have a noticeably lower sex ratio in the age cohort of 0-4 years (78.26), but in succeeding age cohorts, the age specific sex-ratios tend to increase. So, approximately 22 numbers of female children per 100 male children are missing in the population at that calendar year. One of the reasons for such a dismal picture may be negligence towards the female children. It is told by the

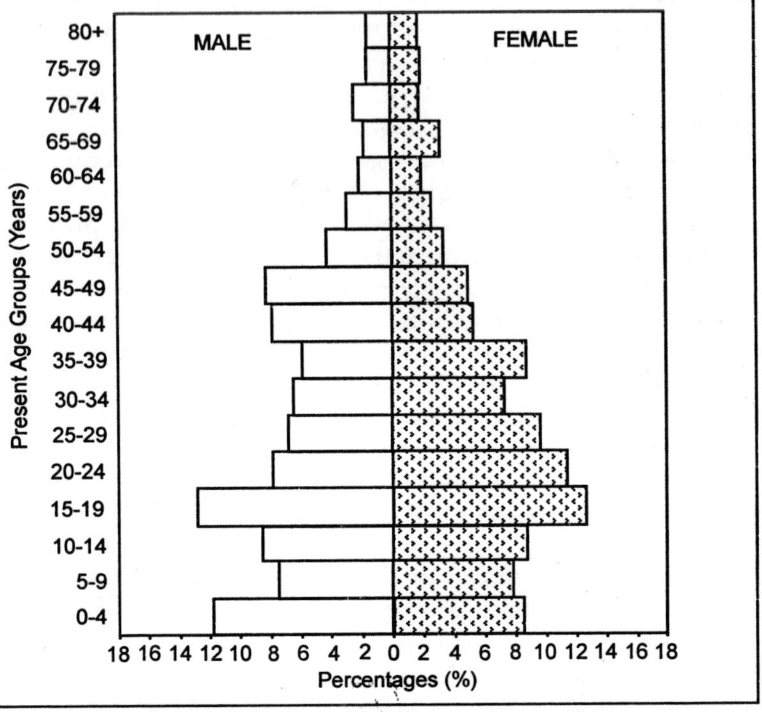

Fig 7.1: Population Pyramid of the Mishings of Kumarbari

village ASHA workers that the female children are rarely taken to the nearby PHC when they fall sick. They had to suffer from relatively more episodes of diarrhoea or other form of illness to be taken to the PHC than their male counterparts.

Family planning means having the desired number of children and when to have them. So it is very essential to know the advantages that a married couple can gain through this process. In the present study, it has been found that the husbands mostly act as decision makers of accepting family planning methods. But no other family members except the wife and the husband are concerned in taking decisions for acceptance of family planning methods. It has been found that the couples often gather knowledge regarding family planning methods from their friends, relatives as well as very recently from the ASHA workers of the village. The age-wise distribution of women according to acceptor and non-acceptor of various family planning devices (Table 7.2)

Table 7.1: Distribution of Mishing Population by Age and Sex of Kumarbari Village, Majuli

Current Age-Group (years)	Males		Females		Total		Sex Ratio
	No.	%	No.	%	No.	%	
0-4	69	11.75	54	8.54	123	10.09	78.26
5-9	44	7.50	49	7.75	93	7.63	111.36
10-14	50	8.52	55	8.70	105	8.61	110.00
15-19	75	12.78	80	12.66	155	12.71	106.67
20-24	46	7.83	72	11.39	118	9.68	156.52
25-29	40	6.81	61	9.65	101	8.29	152.50
30-34	38	6.47	46	7.28	84	6.89	121.05
35-39	35	5.96	55	8.70	90	7.46	157.14
40-44	46	7.83	33	5.22	79	6.48	71.74
45-49	48	8.18	31	4.91	79	6.48	64.58
50-54	25	4.26	21	3.32	46	3.77	84.00
55-59	17	2.90	16	2.53	33	2.71	94.12
60-64	12	2.04	12	1.90	24	1.97	100.00
65-69	10	1.70	12	3.16	22	1.80	120.00
70-74	14	2.39	15	1.74	29	2.38	107.14
75-79	9	1.53	9	1.90	18	1.48	100.00
80+	9	1.53	11	1.74	20	1.64	122.22
Total	**587 (48.15%)**	**100.00**	**632 (51.85%)**	**100.00**	**1219**	**100.00**	**107.67**

Table 7.2: Age-Wise Distribution of Women According to Acceptor and Non-Acceptor of Various Family Planning Devices

Current Age Groups (years)	Mishing Women		
	No. of Women	Acceptor	Non-Acceptor
Below 19	–	–	–
20-24	10	60.00	40.00
25-29	23	86.96	13.04
30-34	24	70.83	29.17
35-39	37	29.73	70.27
40-44	19	36.84	63.16
45-49	19	15.79	84.21
50-54	19	–	100.00
55-59	10	–	100.00
60-64	18	–	100.00
65+	21	–	100.00
Total	**200**	**36.50**	**63.50**

shows that the women who are currently at the age group of 45-49 years are the women who initiated the utilization of family planning measures when they were in the reproductive span. At the present time, the range of age of acceptor women among the population is found to be 21-42 years. Though 3.25 per cent of women are found to be married at the age below 19 years but they did not use any kind of family planning devices. It is also evident that the number of acceptors increases with the decreasing age of the women. This suggests that more and more number of women are informed about the benefits of family planning measures in the younger age cohorts. The younger generation of couples expresses the desire to limit the family size to two sons and a daughter and would have a fourth child only if all the three children happened to be sons or *vice versa*. It is interesting to note here that though 87.0 per cent of women are aware of/heard of family planning as a process to limit the number of children but only 4.91 per cent know the fact that by accepting family planning measures they can have adequate and desired spacing between two successive births; only 8.09 per cent of women are aware of these two benefits of family planning. It is interesting that though all the women to some extend have heard of family planning measures but a few women (36.50%) have accepted these actually during some point of time in their reproductive span (Table 7.4). In the last five years, the ASHA workers make these devices available to the women.

Analysis of the present status shows that the husbands mostly act as decision makers of family planning measures and also decide the number of children they should have. When the women respondents were asked whether they plan the gap between two successive births, 87.2 per cent responded that it is rarely discussed among the spouses and they accept whatever their husbands decide. The concept of composition of ideal family size is an important socio-cultural factor that may control the fertility of a couple. The concept of 'ideal family' of a couple may be based on

Table 7.3: Respondents' Response to 'Why Family Planning'?

Responses	*Percentage*
Limiting the number of children (Only)	87.0
Birth Spacing (Only)	4.91
Both	8.09

Table 7.4: Distribution of Couples Accepting Various Family Planning Methods and Devices

Family Planning Devices	*Mishing Women*	
	No. of Couples	%
Tubectomy	15	7.50
Vasectomy	6	3.00
Oral contraceptive pill	22	11.00
IUCD	16	8.00
Condom	3	1.50
Oral contraceptive pill and condom	4	2.00
Oral contraceptive pill and iucd	7	3.50
Total acceptors	73	36.50
Total non-acceptors	127	63.50
Total	**200**	**100.00**

the number and gender composition of the children. The idea of ideal family size is always influenced by certain socio-cultural factors. In them, it is found that the couples wish to continue procreation until they beget atleast two sons.

Table 7.5 presents the distribution of women based on their concept of composition of ideal family size, i.e., desired numbers of sons and daughters. The highest number of Mishing women desire a family composed of three sons and two daughters, followed by the number of women who desire two sons and two daughters in their ideal family size of five or four children. It is apparent from the table that most of the Mishing women desire at least two or three sons in their family. It is interesting to note here that a considerable number of Mishing women (17.0%) desire two sons and one daughter in their ideal family size. Among them,

Table 7.5: Concept of Composition of Ideal Family Size

Composition of Ideal Family	*Mishing Women*	
	No.	%
One Son and One Daughter	6	3.00
Two Sons and One Daughter	34	17.00
Two Sons and Two Daughters	63	31.50
Three Sons and Two Daughters	70	35.00
Four Sons and Two Daughters	17	8.50
Three Sons and Three Daughters	10	5.00
God's Wish	–	–
Total	**200**	**100.00**

Table 7.6: Desired Number of Children Among the Mishing Women

Current Age Groups (Years)	*Mishing Women*			
	Total No. Women	*No. of Women Depend on God's Wish or No Comment*	*No. of Respondents*	*Average Ideal Number of Children*
20-24	10	–	10	3.10
25-29	23	–	23	3.62
30-34	24	3	21	4.00
35-39	37	6	31	4.45
40-44	19	9	10	5.00
45-49	19	8	11	5.23
50-54	19	11	8	5.67
55-59	10	8	2	5.50
60-64	18	16	2	5.50
65+	21	19	2	6.00
Total	**200**	**82**	**118**	**4.81**

the total average desired number of children (4.81) is found to be slightly higher than the average fertility (4.78). The present study reveals an inverse relationship between the average desired number of children and the educational status of women. Sundar (1990) states that education decreases the demand or desire for more children and increases the use of contraception, thereby reducing fertility. It is evident from the present study that the average number of desired children is higher among the illiterate and barely literate women than the women with higher educational levels. The older and illiterate women had non-numeric response towards the desired number of children like, "conception depends on the wish of God (*Donyi: Polo*)." It is revealed that like any other patriarchal societies, the Mishings too desire sons more strongly than the daughters. The strong preference for son is clearly evident as the highest numbers of women (more than half) desires to have at least two sons and they wish to continue procreation until they beget two sons (Table 7.7). For them, the birth of a son/sons seems more important than the daughters. They try to ensure that if something unfortunate happens to one of the sons than the other one survives to do their last rites after death and to propagate their clan and lineage. However, it is pertinent to note here that the Mishings also welcome daughters but either one or two and not more than that. According to the respondents, a daughter is

Table 7.7: Distribution of Couples According to Values Regarding Additional Child if the First Child is a Daughter

Values Regarding Additional Child if the First Child is a Daughter	*Mishing Women*	
	No.	%
Continue Until Birth of One Son	27	13.50
Continue Until Birth of Two Sons	102	51.00
Continue Until Birth of Two Sons and One More Daughter	46	23.00
Continue Until Birth of Three Sons or More	7	3.50
God's wish	7	3.50
No Comment	11	5.50
Total	**200**	**100.00**

necessary to help the mother in the household chores and for rearing the younger siblings (preferably sons) when the mothers are in the agricultural field. Their ideal family composition seems to consist of three sons and two daughters or two sons and one daughter (for younger generation of mothers).

More than half of the couples are found to have more than their desired number of children basically because of non-fulfilment of their strong desire to have at least two sons. In Kerela and Andhra Pradesh also the value of a son was found to be an important determinant of high fertility (Mahadevan and Sumangala, 1987). Malhi (1995) found that the fertility in India is influenced by a strong desire to acquire minimum number of surviving sons in the family. Barooah and Iyer (1994) examined religion and fertility in India and found that sons bring benefits to their parents whereas daughters impose costs and is complementing a desire to have sons not to have a daughter. According to Rao *et al.* (1983), couples with a strong preference for sons or at least one son are likely to go beyond their desired family size if their preferences are not achieved. The next cause of having more than desired number of children among the study population is found to be the improper utilization of family planning devices. It has been found that most of the women who adopt copper-T device (IUCD) for family limitation, are unable to use the device correctly or as directed and so they suffer from severe gynaecological ailments like infections and pain quite frequently. Three (03) Mising women reported that they conceived after undergoing tubectomy. As a result, most of the couples do not rely on permanent sterilization.

Among them oral contraceptive pills form the major family planning device followed by IUCDs (Table 7.4). This corroborates with the study by Pandey (2015) who states that the use of IUCD is higher among the rural populations. It is important to note here that though permanent sterilization is used by a very few couples, but it is evident that they tend to prefer tubectomy more than vasectomy. When the respondents were asked as to why they preferred tubectomy over vasectomy, they responded that vasectomy causes physical weakness and impotency among males, in addition to reasons like males cannot take rest for long and have to do strenuous works. Moreover, some of the females responded that if the male children die and the husbands have undergone sterilization then they would not have the chance to procreate again, however, if only the women undergo sterilization then in such case the husbands may marry other women and have son/sons. However, such a kind of instance is not common.

The number of non-acceptors of family planning devices is found to exceed the number of acceptors (Table 7.4). Couples show three reasons for not accepting and practicing any family planning methods and these three reasons are: fear of side effects, desire to have male children and the reduction in coital satisfaction. Side-effects include headache, weight gain, nausea, physical weakness, spontaneous abortion, degeneration of the female genitals and infertility. In addition to these reasons, some of the couples stated that the devices are not very reliable. The strong preference for sons (at least two) is the major reason for not accepting any family planning methods. In order to increase the space between the issues, some women go for abortion by consuming a paste prepared from leaves and roots of *Coptis teeta* (*teeta* in Mising; *mishimi teeta* in Assamese) with raw papaya fruit (*Carica papaya; omita* in Mising; *amita* in Assamese) and powdered bark of *Alstonia scholaris (singar* in Mising; *chatiyana* in Assamese). However, they could not confirm the efficiency of these herbal abortificiants. Abortion is, however, not a very common phenomenon in the communities. It is interesting that the women expect their husband to initiate discussions of family planning as they are the heads of the families. As a result, the inter-spousal communication on family planning is found to be very uncommon.

REFERENCES

Bongaarts, J., Cleland, J., Townsend, J.W., Bertrand, J.T., Das Gupta, M. (2012). *Family Planning Programs for the 21st Century, Rational and Design,* The Population Council, New York.

Borooah, V. and S. Iyer. (2004). *Religion and Fertility in India: The Role of Son.* Preference and Daughter Aversion, SSSR/RRA, Annual Meeting Abstract.

Census of India 2011. Office of the Registrar General and Census Commission, India.

Comparative Study of Men and Women in Haryana. *The Journal of Family Welfare,* 41(2): 53-60.

Decline in Rural Karnataka. Population Research Centre at the Institute for Social and Economic Change, Bangalore.

Device. *Scholars Journal of Applied Medical Sciences.* Vol. 3(1E): 367-372.

Fertility Decline. Sage Publications, New Delhi.

Government of India, Ministry of Home Affairs.

Helzner, J.F. (1996). Men's Involvement in Family Planning, *Reproductive Health Matter,* May(7): 146-54.

Mahadevan, K. and M. Sumangala (1987). *Social Development, Cultural Change and Fertility Decline,* Sage Publication, New Delhi.

Malhi, P. (1995). Influence of Gender Preference for Children on Fertility Behaviour: A *Matters,* May; (7):146-54.

Pandey, D. (2015). Urban Rural Comparison of Side Effect and Removal of Intrauterine *Planning Programmes for the 21st Century.* Rationale and design. The Population Council, New York.

Rao, B., R.M. Kulkarni and P. Hanumantha Rayappa (1983). Determinants of Fertility Results. *The Journal of Family Welfare,* XXXVI(2): 60-68.

Sundar, R. (1990). The Status of Women and Family Planning Acceptance: Some Field Result, *The Journal of Family Welfare,* XXXVI (2), 60-68.

8

Status of Working Women

A Sociological Study Based in a Tea Estate of Assam

Upasana Borthakur

Women work only out of economic necessity to make an additional income to the household expenditure. So women are often treated as secondary earners in the family and they have a dual responsibility of home and workplace. The primary responsibility of women is considered to be the domestic sphere. The fewer opportunities for acquiring appropriate education and skills among women confine them mostly to low paid and unskilled jobs in which they are exploited most by the capitalists. Women workers are low paid with longer hours of work in inhuman working conditions with relatively fringe benefits and are used as a reserve army of labour. But in spite of the economic contribution that a woman makes to the income of the family, she enjoys no respect or status in the family. She is not even allowed to spend the money earned independently. Thus patriarchy and capitalism are working simultaneously as sources of female subordination. Keeping all these in mind the scribe has tried to examine the status of women workers among the tea garden communities. For this purpose 100 women workers were interviewed from a tea estate in Dibrugarh district. The scribe has tried to examine the social life, community life, health, education, working conditions, living conditions, household responsibilities etc. to get an account of their position in the home and workplace both. The conclusions arrived suggest that it is far from the truth that economic independence has given the plantation women workers equal status with men. Though apparently they enjoy considerable freedom, still their overall position in society has remained low. The inequality between men and women extends almost to every sphere of life, in unequal job mobility, unequal occupational and social status. In the patriarchal plantation society there is no special identity for women.

Introduction

Women's work has traditionally been divided into the area of production (both economic and social) and reproduction from time immemorial. With the intensity of specialization, women's work became more segregated and sexual division of labour became a dominant agenda. Their participation in the economy and contribution to household income became more evident. The percentage of working women in India has been increasing constantly over the years. The status of working women in India has changed a lot amidst the years but their vulnerability remains the same. It cannot be denied that even in the 21st century the women still struggling for the hardships which they used to face decades ago. The clout of religion, society, family hinders their growth and affects their personal and professional life. India is still a patriarchal society where there is a domination of men over women be in rural or urban areas women are still struggling to search for their identity. Whether are engaged in agricultural activities or are recruited in top managerial position they have to accomplish their household as well as professional duties at par. Therefore, the pace of growth is very sluggish as they have to contribute their energies equally towards family and work.

The Indian labour market is characterized by very low rates of female labour force participation (Neetha, 2002). Women account for most unpaid work and when women are employed in paid work they are overrepresented in the informal sector. In the overall economic activity in India, women workers constitute about one-fifth of the total workforce, out of which only six per cent are employed in the organized sector (IMF Report, 2015). In spite of legislative provisions, their exploitation exists not only in the unorganized sector but in the organized sector also. There are cases where women workers are deprived of the benefits and amenities like equal remuneration *vis-à-vis* their male counterparts, maternity benefits, proper child care services etc. In many cases women are themselves not aware of their rights. The fewer opportunities for acquiring appropriate education and skills among women workers confine them to mostly low paid and unskilled jobs. Women are often treated as secondary earners in the family and they have a dual responsibility to perform that of home and workplace. The primary responsibility of women is commonly considered to be the domestic sphere.

According to Marxian analysis women's subordination in society is not a result of her biological dispositions but of social relations. The modes of production determine the lives of women within the household both by defining the internal structure of it and by locating their position in the social system. According to Borah (2008), the Marxists interpret the structural location of women in capitalist society. Women wage workers are presumably exploited the same way as wage labourers; they are alienated, low paid with longer hours of work in inhuman working conditions with relatively fringe benefits and used as a reserve army of labour. Thus women's subordination is a function of class oppression, maintained because it serves the interests of the capitalists. But in spite of the economic contribution that a woman worker makes to the income of the family, she enjoys no respect or status in the the family. She is only considered as a secondary earner in the family and her position in society is no different. Thus capitalism and patriarchy are working simultaneously as sources of female subordination

According to Rasaily (2015), women's labour is central to the economies of production; more so in the case of production of plantation commodities such as tea and coffee. One of the remarkable features of plantations is the large number of female workers, who constitute 50 per cent of the total workforce. Employment of women in plantations historically was sought by the planters in order to contain the male labour force and to ensure a steady reproduction of cheap labour as recruitment costs were expensive. Quite plausibly the planters saw women adapting well to the plantations most tedious and prolonged labour of tea picking (Guha, 1977). Thus, one of the important features of tea industry in India is the proportionately higher levels of female employment in cultivation and production.

From the above discussion we may derive that the socio-economic status of women workers of various sectors is very poor.

The researcher in order to understand the socio-economic status of the women workers in tea plantation sector conducted an empirical investigation in a tea plantation in Dibrugarh district in Assam. The name of the garden is Achabam located near Naharkatiya town. This garden was originally owned and managed by British Company but now-a-days this is managed by Tata Group of Industries. The researcher found that the tea estate has 400 permanent workers out of which 200 are male and 200 are female. There is total of eight labour lines which are Natun Line, Kallar Line, Ek Number Line, Pakka Line, Bazaar Line, Das Number Line, Maslipatti Line, Chowkidar Line and Bombay line. The researcher by purposive sampling selected 100 women workers from five labour lines and conducted personal interview with them in the month of October 2016. The major findings of the study are enumerated below.

Social Security Benefits of Women Workers in Tea Plantations

The conditions of plantation workers are statutorily governed by the Plantation Labour Act, 1951, and also a host of other labour enactments. This Act is a Central legislation administered by State Governments through rules framed by them. The Plantation Labour Act covers both conditions of work and living conditions. The Plantation Labour Act requires the employer to provide to the workers and their family members housing, medical, sickness and education facility and various other social security benefits. The author in this work has tried to probe into the health, education, crèche, housing, ration and other facilities provided by the management of Achabam tea estate. Article 46 of the Assam Plantation Rules of 1956, provides that in every plantation wherein 50 or more women workers are employed, the employer shall provide and maintain crèches for the use of the children. The Achabam crèche was established in 1985 and there are 253 children in the crèche who are in the age group of 2 to 6 years. The crèche has eight staff out of which six are female staff. The crèche attendant and two community health visitors were trained in special training for working in crèche. Besides these they also have to make visits to the labour lines to pick up children for crèche and to increase awareness among people about their children. The children in the crèche are provided with nutritional food and milk. Some mothers whose children are below 2 years come to crèche to feed their children with milk. The only complaint among the permanent women workers in the crèche is that they are getting the same daily rate as that of women plucking in the tea estate. But according to them they are doing more hard work than the women pluckers. Most of the women workers send their children to school while going to work. Some women leave their children in home as there is someone to look after their children.

Section 14 of the Plantation Labour Act, 1951 states that where the children between the age of six and twelve years of the workers employed in any plantation exceed 25 in number, the state government may make rules requiring every employer to provide educational facilities for the children in such manner and of such standard as may be prescribed. There is one lower primary school in Achabam tea estate which was established in 1957. There is another lower primary school in the Achabam tea estate premises, Achabam Navajyoti established in 1981. Uniforms, books and mid-day meal facilities are provided by the Sarva Sikhsa Abhiyan. Besides there are three Anganbari centres in Achabam tea estate premises. Regarding the education of the women workers, most of the women are illiterate or can write their names only. The reason for their illiteracy was their parent's indifference attitude towards their daughter's education. But now-a-days most of the women workers send their children to school and as many as 10 per cent parents were found concerned about their children's education.

In Achabam tea estate the garden hospital was established in 1942. The permanent workers get medical facility free of cost. The women workers get maternal health care during pre- and post-delivery. So most of the childbirths have taken place in hospital. The women workers are suffering from various diseases, anaemia and tuberculosis are the worst hit diseases among the women workers. Besides many women get married at an early age and get pregnant easily as they are not aware of contraceptives. Thus maternal mortality and infant mortality are common among women workers. There are many superstitious beliefs among the women workers and they rely more on homemade medicines (*jangli darab*) for full cure of their illness. There are many cases where women workers after completing the medical course take recourse to homemade medicines.

The Achabam tea management provides housing facilities to

the workers. The houses are *Pacca,* i.e. made of brick walls, cement floors and C.I. Sheet roofing. Most of the labour quarters are now repaired and newly constructed by the workers themselves. The Plantation Labour Act, 1951, has a provision for adequate supply of drinking water for the workers and also provides for sanitary latrines. In Achabam tea estate every labour quarter has a tubewell and a latrine provided by the management. But there is no bathroom facility for the women workers.

The Wages of Women Workers

Wages in the plantation industry varied from place to place. Wages are both based on piece and time rates. The wage workers are to work eight hours in a day and six days in a week. The *hazira* or daily wage is paid to a worker on completion of task allotted for the day. *Ticca* is paid for any extra task or work and for overtime work. In Achabam tea estate the daily *hazira* of a woman worker is Rs. 126 and it is paid twice in a month, i.e. every 15 days work. The amount of leaves to be plucked by a worker is 24 kgs for daily *hazira*. And they are paid additional Rs. 2 for an extra kilo plucked. Earlier women used to get fewer wages than their male counterparts but after 1976 with the Equal Remuneration Act the wage differentials were abolished. Besides this the workers are also getting provident fund and some per cent of money is deducted from their salary. The workers are also getting bonus once in a year. The women workers are also getting maternity leave for three months. After three months when they join they are given *aaya* (nanny) who look after their children in the garden when they pluck leaves. The workers get ration at concessional rates. Some protective uniforms which are essential for working in the plantation are also supplied free to the workers. Apron, umbrella and sandals are such articles. Each worker receives from the authority a blanket once in every two years free of cost.

The Nature of Women's Work

The entire workforce in Achabam tea estate is divided in two broad categories: workers and staff. The bulk of the workforce constitutes the former category while the latter group is few in number. The daily wage workers perform all types of manual work such as plucking of leaves, weeding, transplanting, hoeing, manuring, forking and cleaning soil, pruning tea bushes, taking care of nursery bed of young tea plants and cleaning of tea stalks in the factory. The period from May to November is generally regarded as the busy season in tea plantations, July to September is the peak period of the plucking season and the workers specially the women can earn entire wages from plucking over the required norm. December to March is the slack season in plantations when the earning of women workers as well as average earning of a family remains generally low. The pruning which is an important operation is done by young and efficient women workers. The work in which women are generally employed are plucking of leaf. In the tea factory aged and weak women are employed in picking out stalks from the tea leaves.

Generally all those who work in plantations are done in groups under the supervision of Dafadars and Sardars. Each group is consisted of about fifty workers either men or women. The Sardars who are always males, supervise in plucking of leaves. The women tea pluckers work from morning 8 to 4 pm. During this period they have to pluck 24kgs of tea leaves only then they will get their *hazira*. In Achabam tea estate there are three weighting times and the workers get one hour resting time. Drinking water and tea is provided by the management to the workers during working hours. But there is no resting shed for the workers. The workers generally take shade under big trees and have their lunch which they bring from home. There is no toilet facility for the workers. But the workers are treated immediately if any accident happens while at work. The workers reported to the investigator that they are prone to various incest bites or also snakes if they are not conscious while plucking leafs. The Sardars are also always under their head and they cannot even talk with others while at work. The workers also consider their wages very less as it becomes very difficult for them to make both ends meet.

Women and Job Mobility within Plantations

The workers in the tea plantations are usually classified into categories of staff according to hierarchy. In Achabam tea estate all employees can be differentiated into four categories: managerial staff, office staff, sub-staff and workers. The managerial staff includes the Manager and two Assistant Managers. The office staff includes the office clerical staff, medical, educational and welfare department staff. The sub-staff includes the artisans and technicians, sardars and chowkidars etc. No woman has been appointed to occupy a position neither in the managerial category nor in the sub-staff category. The office staff is recruited from both men and women. The nature of duties of the supervisory workers is considered unsuitable for women. The sub-staff is generally promoted from the ordinary workers and only men workers are considered eligible for such promotions. Women workers are deprived of such promotion opportunities. All the sub-staff draws monthly wages and they are regarded as superior to the ordinary workers as they get little higher wages. But the ordinary workers get daily wages. The women workers are never found to be appointed to posts relating to the managerial, executive work nor are they employed in the clerical or allied positions. Practically the women workers have no facility for promotion. In every stratum of the plantation hierarchy men have monopolized more responsible positions, which are often better paid.

The women workers are significantly more satisfied with their wages than the men workers. The women workers in spite of being recognized as committed workers cannot move up in the job hierarchy. The men workers can move up to occupy positions of Sardars, Dafadar, Boider, Chowkidar, Chaprashi and Munshi. But the women workers never protest for such discrimination simply because their expectation out of employment is limited. Their socialization process also helps them to accept the plantation occupation as their family occupation and has made them unconcerned about their low position in the industry. The low level of education of the women workers is positively related to their low occupational aspirations. But in Achabam tea estate the researcher found three women working in office—two in medical department and one in education department. One tribal woman is in the garden hospital occupying the position of Auxiliary Nurse and the other women is Health Assistant in the garden hospital. One other woman is working as a teacher in the Achabam Primary School. Only these three women were found by the scribe whose educational level was Higher Secondary standard while the majority of women were illiterate or at best primary school pass.

Employment being family based automatically restricts the choice of occupation and better standard of living.

The planters prefer to employ women as they think that they are more committed to men. The employers provide some facilities which have made the conditions of employment more favourable to the workers. As the workers live within the plantation obviously they have little difficulty in meeting the twin demands of society and plantation industry. It appears that their social life outside the work and their work within the plantations are an integral part of the same world rather than separate spheres of activity. All these facilitities are not generally available in industries other than those of the plantation.

The Family

Out of the 100 families there are 60 nuclear and the rest joint families. I also found some instances where a man has two wives living together in the same house with their children. The most common type of nuclear family has four members. The joint families generally have two generations living together. The workers generally prefer the nuclear families as certain facilities such as free quarter, free firewood, free cultivable land, ration at subsidized rates are given to each family. This naturally encourages the workers to form nuclear families. In many cases these are the factors responsible for spitting up of large joint families into their constituent nuclear families. Moreover, the labour quarters provided to the workers have only 2 rooms and one kitchen. This accommodation is not sufficient for larger households. If there is any family where two adult persons are workers, say for example, a father and a son who live together, they are entitled to get one quarter only. If a son gets married he is entitled to get a separate quarter. The plantation society is patriarchal in nature so the authority of the family rests in the hands of the male member of the family.

Sharing of Household Responsibilities and Decision Making

In traditional Hindu society allocation of household functions and responsibilities is distinct between husband and wife. This distinction has given rise to specialization of duties among them, such as, wife looks after all the domestic work and rearing up of children, the husband earns for the maintenance of the family. The former's duties are confined to the domestic activities while the latter's duties are largely outside the home. But in the plantation society both husband and wife work together and most husbands equally participate in domestic activities. Thus they share each other's economic and domestic responsibilities. The sharing of household responsibility is principally found in the spheres of three domestic activities: handling of family purse to meet regular expenses, performance of daily domestic chores and looking after the children. It is natural that when the wife is working as wage earner she has a dual burden to carry. It was found that majority of the husband help their wives in domestic activities. In the plantation society doing the domestic chores and looking after the children do not affect the dignity of the husband. One of the indicators of status of women is whether they play an effective role in the decision making process in the family and whether they can spend the women earned independently. About 70 per cent of the women workers mentioned that they play important role in the decision making in their family. Though majority of the working women desire in decision making, in actual practice this is enjoyed by a very few of them. In certain vital issues in the family like marriage and education of sons and daughters, husbands usually unilaterally take the decision. Wives' opinion is not much valued. But the wives take the major decisions regarding the day to day family expenditure, domestic activities, etc. As the wives spend all of their wages for the maintenance of the family they have a greater say in the day to day affairs of the family.

Alcoholism and Domestic Violence

Alcoholism is a truth in almost every tea tribe family in Assam. Everyone is familiar with and yet is unable to escape from its pitfalls. In Achabam tea estate 90 per cent of the women's husbands are alcoholic. Most of the husbands spend a part of their earnings on drinking rice beer (*Haria*) and *Sulai* (local wine). Rice beer is prepared in the labour lines and sold by the labourers themselves. In Achabam tea estate there is one labour line called Kallar line which is famous for sale of *Haria*. The men workers after coming from work consume *Haria* in the evening as they are tired after whole day's hard labour. But the women workers after coming from work do all the household works and look after children. There is no leisure time for women at all. Alcoholism is so rampant in Achabam tea estate that it results in domestic violence. Majority of the women are victims of domestic violence. The women workers mentioned that majority of the fights take place when their husbands are drunk as they are not in their senses.

The Marriage

In the tribal society marriage appears to be more a social contract based on individual choice, rather than a sacrament. A boy and a girl can marry according to their own will without prior consent of their parents. Endogamous marriage is the general rule, though there are numerous cases of inter tribal marriages. Although marriage is strictly monogamous, sometimes polygamy also takes place. The consensual union when a couple live together without being married is very common. Majority of the women workers told this investigator that they eloped. If they are from a different *jati* (caste) then they must first by rituals enter into the *jati* only then they can enter kitchen and prayer house as their wives. The real marriage or *Sindurdaan* takes place later even after the birth of children if the marriage formalities prove to be burdensome at a given point of time. In two instances the researcher found that *Sindurdaan* ceremony of daughter-in-law and mother-in-law taking place together. In another instance the researcher found that her husband died when her children were small but their *Sindurdaan* did not take place. If the parents do not perform their own marriage rituals their children do not get legitimacy. Plantation communities try to confine affinal relations within their group from the neighbouring plantations. But due to economic interests now-a-days most of the marriages take place within the same plantations. The job opportunities of a worker are very limited today. If a girl is married to a boy of other plantation she will have to leave her job. Since, there is no guarantee for getting regular job in other tea plantations, girls as well as their parents are more inclined to settle their marriages in the same tea plantation.

Another thing the scribe found is that they are religious people and followers of traditions. The women workers wake up early in the morning and do all household works. They enter kitchen or cook food only after taking bath. The veil system or covering the head before elders is very common among them. They do not even sit in equal height with elders. They are also very religious. Even if they are busy they take out time and do evening and morning *puja* regularly. Besides these many *pujas* and festivals are celebrated in home. Thus the tribal women are still holding to their traditions.

Political Participation of Women Workers

The All Assam Mazdoor Sangha branch is working in Achabam tea estate. A certain amount of money is deducted from the workers whether temporary or permanent in the name of donation for this trade union. It has a total of 50 members in the trade union with only 7 women members. The Executive Committee of this union consists of Secretary, President and other 5 members. No woman is a member of this Executive Committee. Most of the women the researcher interviewed were unaware of this trade union and so participation in trade union is out of question. Some of the women reported the investigator that the meetings of trade union were held in the evening so it becomes difficult for them to attend meetings as they have to do household works. The women who were members of this trade union also told the researcher that earlier the management used to give them half day leave with pay to attend meetings of trade union which were generally held in the afternoon. It was convenient for women at that time. There is another women's organization in this tea estate called Mother's Club which has 20 members. Generally the women who are educated become members of trade union or mother's club. So most of the women interviewed were even unaware of this Mother's club. The mother's club work for women workers and organize awareness camps about health, hygiene and sanitation and also take out processions in the labour lines about the ill effects of *haria* and alcohol. Thus, it was found that in Achabam tea estate there is very low participation of women in the trade union activities. Most of the women also mentioned that their husbands do not allow them to attend the public meetings of trade union.

Conclusion

From the above discussion, the question that looms large is that whether economic emancipation of women workers has correspondingly elevated their status in the society or not. Traditionally in caste society the status of women was generally lower, whereas in tribal society it was relatively higher. One of the factors which contributes to a higher status of women in tribal society is the economic role that they perform as wage earners. But it will be wrong to assume that the women workers in plantation industry enjoy equal rights and privileges with men. It is true that tribal women workers suffer few restrictions in their society. They can select their mates and can leave their mates as and when they like or they can marry again. They do not have system of dowry. But still tribal society is male dominated and women are treated as a commodity.

The overall occupational status of the women workers is lower than that of men workers. Although wages of men and women workers are equal today, even a few years ago the latter used to receive lesser wages. There is a still unequal opportunity in occupation between men and women in plantation. Women are never promoted to any higher position and therefore, they have to remain as daily wage workers throughout their life. The plantation women workers do not have any role to perform in the decision making process with regard to important affairs of the family. Trade union leadership from among women has not yet emerged. Although women workers are members of trade union they hardly participate in the union activities. Educational attainment of women workers is also very low. This has further helped to perpetuate the lower status of women workers. They are totally ignorant about the role of modern education in improving the status of women. Thus economic contribution has not helped to raise their status so as to make it equal with men.

Though there is no rigid compartmentalization of work for male and female workers some sort of division of labour exists in plantation. The women workers perform their assigned tasks sincerely and skillfully. They enjoy employment benefits which are equal to those received by men workers. In addition they receive maternity benefits. But in the plantation hierarchy men have monopolized all the responsible positions, although among the daily wage workers women outnumber men. Nevertheless the tribal women are highly committed to the plantation work. They are basically propelled by their economic motivation. In general their expectations and aspirations are very low due to their traditional cultural background, low economic condition, poor educational level etc.

There is a trend of nuclearisation of tribal family which is evident from its predominance in the society. Certain factors are responsible for splitting up of joint families into smaller ones. These are recruitment policies, facilities for quarter and ration provided by the plantation management. Majority of the husbands extend helping hands to their wives in housekeeping tasks. But they do not have a say in the important affairs of the family, major decisions of family are usually taken by husbands. In the plantation most of the women workers are accommodative as their work demands can be fitted into their family requirements. They integrate work and family in their daily life without any visible strain. In the tea industry both the residential and working sectors are within the same area. Thus a woman can without strain fulfil the roles as a wife, mother and worker. The participation of women in work does not adversely affect interpersonal relationships between husband and wife. But only alcoholism creates situation of conflict between husband and wife which sometimes results in domestic violence also.

It is far from the truth that economic independence has given the plantation women an equal status with men. Though apparently they enjoy considerable freedom, still their overall position in society has remained low. The inequality between men and women extends to almost every sphere of life, in unequal job mobility, wage rate, unequal occupational and social status. In the patriarchal plantation society there is special status for women. Even the capital intensive plantation industry is not giving any occupational mobility to the women workers. The women workers because of low level of education have no high aspirations and are happy with their work and working conditions. Thus the management is satisfied with the women workers as they are easy to administer. The ignorance, lack of skill and assertive nature makes them subservient both at the place of work and family life.

REFERENCES

Bhadra, Mita (1985). "Women workers in tea plantations", *Indian Anthropologist*, Vol. 15, No. 2.

Borah, Putul (2008). *The Dynamics of Labour Exploitation: Tea Plantation Labour in Assam*, unpublished M.Phil. Dissertation submitted to the Department of Sociology, Delhi University.

Jain, Shobita (1988). *Sexual Equality: Workers in an Asian Plantation System*, New Delhi: Sterling Publishers.

Kaniampady, Elizabeth (2003). *Status of Women Working in Tea Plantation*, Akanksha Publishing House, Assam.

Neetha, N. (2002). "Flexible Production, Feminization and Disorganization: Evidence from Tripurram Knitwear Factory," *Economic and Political Weekly*, Vol. 37, No. 21.

Rasaily, Rinju (2014). *Women's Labour in the tea sector: Changing trajectories and emerging challenges*, National Research Programme on Plantation Development (NRPPD).

9

Dalit Women

A Case of Three Tier Discrimination

Parijat Pradhan

Social change, development and Social transformation are the new facets of goal for any country's advancement. When a country neglects these parameters of progress or development in holistic or inclusive manner, it will surely seize in the coming generations. The major resource or strength of any country is its socially accountable, rational and democratic citizens. The states of that country have also to ensure and to look upon the rights, social justice, empowerment and other necessary access to opportunities of the citizens through various laws and means. Especially the Indian subcontinent has ensured the equality for all by framing certain laws, by providing certain fundamental rights and by passing various Acts under the Constitution of India.

Every year our country is achieving new success stories in international markets, in educational sectors, in health infrastructure, in high GDP rates etc. through our manpower. We have enjoyed more than 70 years of Indian independence bypassing all past exploitations, sufferings, deprivations etc. But the biggest question is, whether we have really achieved the target of "Equality to All", does our whole sections of the country are getting access to all avenues and opportunities, can we really say that all social evils have no say just by passing laws and regulations, are we really making an inclusive society and for all. We have laws for weaker sections of the country, but still they are facing discriminations, sufferings, exploitations in all sectors of the society. Caste conflicts and honour killings have become stronger in the era of identity politics where reservation has become a weapon and tool to make easy equations. Gender discriminations have become a menace in every country with various new subtle forms like trafficking, murder after rape, female foeticide, eve teasing, groping etc. And if we take the case of *Dalit* women, then it is a case of triple edged discrimination where caste, gender and class all are playing their nefarious roles. Further, *Dalit* feminists have formulated the position of the three-way oppression of *Dalit* women:

- As subject to caste oppression at the hands of the upper castes;
- As labourers subject to the class based oppression, also mainly at the hands of the upper and middle castes who form the bulk of landowners; and
- As women who experience patriarchal oppression at the hands of all men, including men of their own caste.

The hardships of *Dalit* women are not simply due to their poverty, economic status or lack of education, but are a direct result of the severe exploitation and suppression by the upper classes, which is legitimizes by Hindu religious scriptures (Thind, 1995; Agrawal, 1999). Manorma Ruth, an active member of the National Campaign on *Dalit* Human Rights and the National Alliance of Women, once stated that in a male dominated society, "*Dalit* women face a triple burden of caste, class and gender" in which she sums up the plight of *Dalit* women, highlighting the fact that *Dalit* women are a "distinct social group and cannot be masked under the general categories of "*Women*" or "*Dalits*". (*News Archives*).

In Ancient India (3200–2500 B.C.), the caste system was non-existent since even the most learned men were good householders and had varied occupations. The women of ancient India were just as superior as men in learning, education, and intellect. The choice for her mate was according to her own wishes and marriage was practiced after the coming of age. She attended parties, competitions, and religious functions as she wished. The remarriage of young widows was also a common practice (Thind, 1995). The creation of a number of Hindu religious books including the *Manusmriti, Atharva Veda, Vishnu Smriti,* and many others like these and their strict compliance by the *Brahmans* (upper priestly Hindu caste), led to a society in which equality between men and women was far from existent (Agarwal, 1999). Dr. B.R. Ambedkar, an architect of the Constitution of India, also makes it very clear in his article titled *"The Rise and Fall of Hindu Woman"* that the root cause of suffering for women in India are these so called Hindu religious books (Thind, 1995; Agarwal, 1999). Books like the *Manusmriti* divide people into a stratified caste system and promotes inequality between men and women (Thind, 1995; Agarwal, 1999). According to the *Manusmriti*, women have no right to education, independence, or wealth (n.pag). It not only justifies the treatment of *dalit* women as a sex object and promotes child marriage, but also justifies a number of violent atrocities on women as can be seen in the following verses (Agarwal, 1999; *Manusmriti*, 1999):

> "A man, aged thirty years, shall marry a maiden of twelve who pleases him. Or a man of twenty-four a girl of eight years of age. If (the performance of) his duties would otherwise be impeded, he must marry sooner."
>
> (*Manusmriti*, IX. 94)
>
> "By a girl, by a young woman, or even by an aged one, nothing must be done independently, even in her own house." (*Manusmriti*, V. 147)
>
> "Her father protects (her) in childhood, her husband protects (her) in youth, and her sons protect (her) in old age; a woman is never fit for independence."
>
> (*Manusmriti*, IX. 3)
>
> "Women have no right to study the *Vedas*. That is why their *Sanskaras* are performed without *Veda Mantras*. Women have no knowledge of religion because they have no right to know the *Vedas*. The uttering of the *Veda Mantras* is useful for removing sin. As women cannot utter the *Veda Mantras*, they are as unclean as the untruth."
>
> (*Manusmriti*, IX. 18)
>
> "A *Brahman, Kshatriya*, or *Vaishya* Man can sexually exploit any *Shudra* woman." (*Manusmriti*, IX. 25)

Even the killing of a *dalit* woman is explicitly justified as a minor offence for the Brahmins: equal to the killing of an animal (*Manusmriti*). If the killing of an untouchable was justified as a minor offence, you can imagine the treatment they received throughout their lives. Even in Colonial India and in modern times, the status of *Dalit* women has remained the same; though the nature of exploitation varies from physical, verbal to economic exploitation in recent times.

Dalit Women at the Intersection of Multiple Forms of Discrimination

Multiple forms of discriminations mean that overlapping oppression often creates specific forms or ways of experiencing discrimination. Intersectional discrimination multiplies and amplifies the obstacles women face, thus leaving them in a situation of further disadvantage. The intersection of gender discrimination with other barriers (e.g. poverty, caste, rural residence etc.) similarly has a multiplicative effect. It produces something unique and distinct from any one form of discrimination standing alone. 2 *Dalit* women face not just violence (verbal, physical or economic) inflicted on them by the dominant castes, but also state violence, violence at homes and outside. These discriminations being systematic and consistent over a long period are internalised by the *Dalit* woman herself. She accepts the situation as given, and cannot comprehend a life beyond all these discriminations. She is socially conditioned to believe that being a *Dalit* woman this is what her life is as given, and cannot comprehend a life beyond all these discriminations. Powerless and unable to access or control any resources for survival, she undertakes humiliating tedious and time consuming work, mostly without any remuneration, including the most menial and degrading job of manual scavenging as given, and cannot comprehend a life beyond all these discriminations. The better paid and dignified occupations continue to be out of reach for them through a systematic denial of rights to education, training, property rights and other livelihood resources. Literacy rate among *Dalit* women continues to be the lowest at 19.46 per cent. Around 71 per cent of *Dalit* women workers are agricultural labourers. Also around 70 per cent to 75 per cent of *Dalit* families are female headed (Irudayam and Jayshree, NCDHR, 2004). Landlessness is growing at a rapid speed among *Dalits*, as is evident from the fact that the proportion of all *Dalit* workers as agricultural labour is increasingly growing at a very fast rate as compared to the non-*Dalit* agricultural labourers, implying that after losing their land holdings, *Dalit* cultivators are becoming agriculture labourers. One consequence of this is that *Dalit* men migrate to urban areas for better work whilst *Dalit* women are left behind to bear the responsibility of domestic work, care giving as well as work outside in farms and at odd jobs. Absence of males in the family deepens the women's isolation and impoverishment, making them increasingly vulnerable to other forms of discrimination and violence. For example, in absence of any male in the family, men from upper castes threaten and grab land or any other assets from the women (NSS 61st Round, July 2004-June 2005). In absence of any safety nets, and work being very casual, *Dalits*, like the other poor people, are forced to take loans to meet any contingencies such as illnesses, deaths, marriages etc. In their case, given their almost total lack of resources as well as the other caste-based discriminations they face, the upper caste landlord and high interest rates are mostly their only option. This indebtedness becomes an excuse for upper castes to exploit them further in some cases, even making them work as bonded labourers. *Dalit* women in such cases, are most vulnerable to violence included sexual violence and other atrocities. Burdened with work both outside and inside the home, oppressed and excluded socially and economically, *Dalit* women are unable to organise and demand their rights. Compounding this is a fact that groups working on rights generally fail to recognize the triple jeopardy faced by *Dalit* women. In general, when *Dalit* issues are raised, the focus is on caste-based discrimination and the gendered aspects of oppression of *Dalit* women are rendered invisible. Similarly, when women's issues are discussed, caste-based oppression faced by women is left out. Again, whenever *Dalit* women have tried to fight oppression, they are subjected to all kinds of atrocities and violence, including state violence. Vulnerably positioned at the bottom of India's caste, class and gender hierarchies, *Dalit* women experience endemic gender-and-caste discrimination and violence as the outcome of severely imbalanced social, economic and political power equations. Their socio-economic vulnerability and lack of political voice, when combined with the dominant risk factors of being *Dalit* and female, increase their exposure to potentially violent situations while simultaneously reducing their ability to escape. Violence against

Dalit women presents clear evidence of widespread exploitation and discrimination against these women subordinated in terms of power relations to men in a patriarchal society, as also against their communities based on caste. As the National Commission for Women has commented, "in the commission of offences against... Scheduled Caste [*Dalit*] women the offenders try to establish their authority and humiliate the community by subjecting their women to indecent and inhuman treatment, including sexual assault, parading naked, using filthy language etc." Hence, violence, which serves as a crucial social mechanism to maintain *Dalit* women's subordinate position in society, is the core outcome of gender-based inequalities shaped and intensified by the caste system. Atrocities against *Dalit* people are a daily occurrence. The Scheduled caste and Scheduled Tribes (Prevention of Atrocities) Act, 1989 in India defines the type of abuses which are illegal, including:

- Forcing *Dalit* people to eat obnoxious substances;
- Assaulting *Dalit* women with intent to dishonour and outrage her modesty;
- Using a position of dominance to sexually exploit a *Dalit* woman; and
- Corrupting or fouling a *Dalit* water source.

By listing these and other offences, the law reveals the awareness of the many ways in which *Dalit* and Tribal people are subject to indignity, violence and abuse.

It is estimated that a crime is committed against a *Dalit* person every 18 minutes. The problem for many is not the law but the lack of political will, at local and national levels, to apply it. In 2006, the official conviction rate for *Dalit* atrocity cases was just 5.3 per cent.

The statistics are horrifying:

- In rural areas, 37.8 per cent of government run schools make *Dalit* children sit separately from other children;
- In 27.6 per cent of rural villages, *Dalits* are prevented from entering police stations;
- In 33 per cent of rural villages, public health workers refuse to enter *Dalit* homes;

- 48.4 per cent of *Dalit* villages are denied access to water sources; and
- In 70 per cent of rural villages, *Dalit* and non-*Dalit* people cannot eat together.

In rural India, 70 per cent of *Dalit* women are illiterate. In the Southern States, thousands of girls are forced into prostitution before they reach puberty. Temple prostitutes or *Joghinis* (literally 'female servants of God') are usually *Dalit*. Once dedicated, the girl is unable to marry, forced to become a prostitute for upper caste members and eventually auctioned off to an urban brothel (Lenten Study, 2010).

Forms and Frequency of Violence

Twelve major forms of violence constitute the basis of rural areas, nine being violence in the general community—physical assault, verbal abuse, sexual harassment and assault, rape, sexual exploitation, forced prostitution, kidnapping and abduction, forced incarceration and medical negligence—and three being violence in the family—female foeticide and infanticide, child sexual abuse and domestic violence from natal and marital family members (National Campaign for Dalit Human Rights, March 2006). The more frequent forms of violence that are perpetrated against the majority of *Dalit* women are verbal abuse (62.4% of total women), physical assault (54.8%), sexual harassment and assault (46.8%), domestic violence (43.0%) and rape (23.2%), in descending order. Although the remaining forms of violence are faced by relatively fewer *Dalit* women (less than 10% of total women per form of violence), this does not discount their gravity, precisely because of the qualitative factor of force present in these forms of violence (National Campaign for Dalit Human Rights, March 2006). The increasing visibility of *Dalit* women in power structures as Sarpanch or member of the Panchayat and in the new knowledge making processes has led to increased backlash against *Dalit* women. The reason behind this is the growing fear and frustration of the old champions of dogmatic tradition who want to see women in chains and behind the doors. The backlash is expressed through a range of humiliating practices and often culminates in rape, or hacking to death of their kinsmen. Thus, the harm caused to *Dalit* women by violence does not stop at the act itself; it has long-term and multiplying social, psychological and physical effects that are not being addressed. Outside of the social movements and organisations working with the community, little supportive or counselling mechanisms exist in India today to deal with caste-and-gender based violence meted out to *Dalit* women. The result is that the lives of many *Dalit* women are underwritten by layers of trauma, hindering their rights to live with dignity and reach their full potential. The 1992-93 Annual report from the Ministry of Welfare shows 1,236 reported cases of rape on *Dalit* women and the National Commission for SC/ST shows that approximately 10,000 cases of human right violations on *Dalits* are reported every month. But what is even more disturbing, is that only one out of ten of the cases are reported annually whilst, nine go unreported. In addition to this, according to the Human Right watch Report, approximately 115 million children are in slavery and 2.6 million children are held as bonded labourers (Narula, S. 1999). After fifty-five years of India's independence and despite the excellent laws in place to protect *Dalit* women, they are still suffering unimaginable atrocities from the high caste Hindus. It is believed that thousands of these cases go unreported and unpublicized because the poor *Dalits* that live in rural areas, who are the worst victims, have no control on power, wealth, justice, police and the media (Thind, 1995n. pag). The only way these *Dalit* women can escape the vicious cycle of poverty, abuse and oppression is through education. Through education more *Dalit* women can come to know their basic human rights and they can then raise an even stronger voice against abuse and exploitation from the upper castes (Thind; Agarwal). According to the National Commission for Scheduled Castes and Scheduled Tribes 2000, approximately 75 per cent of the *Dalit* girls drop-out of primary schools despite the strict laws of the Government of India, which hold reservations for *Dalit* children (National Commission n. pag). Despite showing keen academic aptitude, reasons for this early drop-out from the education system is poverty or to escape humiliation, bullying and isolation by classmates, society, and even their teachers (Thind, 1995). According to the National Commission for Scheduled Castes and Scheduled Tribes, the majority of the educated people are of the upper caste, many of which may practice caste-based discrimination. Therefore, *Dalit* girls feel discouraged to enter education and we see the lowest literacy rate for *Dalit* girls compared to the Total population of educated upper caste girls (National Commission n. pag). The Annual Report of University Grant Commission for 1999-2000, shows that *Dalits* in general have very low participation rates in higher education (Annual Reports of University n. pag). Since, only a small percentage of the total population of *Dalit* women are educated, the fate of the majority is very grim. According to India's Ministry of Labour, 85 per cent of the *Dalit* women have the most formidable occupations and work as agricultural labourers, scavengers, sweepers, and disposers of human waste. Many of these women work for minimal wages under the upper caste landlords, since it is proposed that by the National Commission for SC/ST that 85 per cent of the *Dalits* are landless (*News Archives*). When the *Dalit* women refuse to work for ridiculously low wages or fail to follow their harsh orders it results open violence, humiliation, beatings, rape, and jail. There are also a number of cases where the houses of *Dalit* women have been burnt down (Agarwal; *News Archives*). Violence against *Dalit* women causes social, physical and mental trauma to women, much of which is long-term suffering. Where violence is committed with impunity, aided by the failure of the police to effect arrests and prosecutions, the fact of the perpetrators and their colluders in the violence freely moving about the village and often intimidating the woman and her family has a deep psychological impact.

Main Challenges for *Dalit* Women in Rural Situations

Caste-affected women in rural settings face a number of serious challenges, including lack of access to resources, land, basic services and justice.

Access to Key Productive Resources

In India, *Dalit* rural women face serious challenges in carrying out their multiple productive and reproductive roles within their families and communities, in part due to lack of rural infrastructure and lack of access to essential goods and services. They have the highest poverty levels, are landless and depend on the dominant caste for employment, wages and loans. Their access to resources or even their efforts to access them are often met with violence.

Due to the intersection of caste, class and gender, *Dalit* women are subjected to direct and structural violence. Specifically, the structural violence and lack of access to resources perpetuate their poverty and undermine their dignity.

Dalit rural women have very limited access to and control over land, which in turn leads to food insecurity. They also lack access to water and other communal resources; when those resources are in non-*Dalit* areas, the women are attacked for attempting to use them. When it comes to infrastructure and resources in *Dalit* communities, the government often overlooks those areas and does not allocate the necessary funds to ensure equality of access to resources. Further, *Dalit* women lack employment options and other livelihood opportunities, more so than their male *Dalit* counterparts.

Women's Access to and Control Over Land

Access to and control over land may be an important factor in attaining food security and an increased income. However, *Dalit* women have limited access to land and no control over it. Due to cultural norms, they do not own land even when it is within their family. Moreover, *Dalits* generally do not own the land but work as agricultural labourer for a dominant caste landlord. The landlords' socio-economic and political power in rural, agricultural areas and status as employers of *Dalit* women allows for continual caste and gender violence, committed with impunity. *Dalit* women are met with physical, verbal and sexual violence from the landlords when they try to assert their economic right to wages or land and their right to sexual integrity. Furthermore, when a *Dalit* woman does have land, she is often accused of being a witch. Witch hunting is a serious problem in rural communities where a *Dalit* woman can be either forced off the land or forced out of the community. The practice is employed as a 'land grab' tactic and is used by non-*Dalits* as well as *Dalits*. This further demonstrates that *Dalit* women are continually met with violence, discrimination and subjugation from every group.

Social Rights and Basic Services

In India, *Dalit* women are often met with violence when attempting to assert their rights in areas such as access to housing, drinking water, the public distribution system (PDS), education or open spaces for open defecation. In a study on 'untouchability' in 1589 villages in Gujarat, the NGO Navsarjan Trust found that *Dalits* were not allowed to fetch water from a tap in a non-*Dalit* area in 71.4 per cent of these villages. In 66.2 per cent of them, non-*Dalit* midwives refused service to *Dalit* women.

One of the many unnecessary hardships of a *Dalit* woman's life is being denied access to basic services, particularly maternal health services. In another study conducted by Navsarjan Trust, the findings showed that 46.5 per cent of *Dalit* women never received the legallyrequired antenatal and postnatal visits. Worse, 54.8 per cent of pregnant women and new mothers from the Valmiki sub-caste, who are traditionally manual scavengers, reported never receiving antenatal or postnatal care visits (Gender-violence and access to justice for the *Dalit* women, Gujarat, India, by Navsarjan Trust, 2011).

Political Participation and Empowerment

Rural women are politically marginalised, but rural *Dalit* women are given even less of a voice in the decision making process. In India, there is a quota system in place for *Dalits* to have seats in the local *panchayat* (town assembly), but the role *Dalit* women play is consistently subordinated to their male counterparts. *Dalit* women who attempt to utilise their power in the *panchayat* are met with male and dominant caste backlash, pressure and sometimes violence. Many times *Dalit* women are told they are not even allowed to sit on a chair, but must take their place on the floor. In the majority of instances a *Dalit* woman has no ability to exercise her voice in the panchayat because her husband represents her and makes the decisions while she is forced to stay at home until he can usurp the panchayat seat for himself.

Violence Against Women, Trafficking, Sexual Exploitation

Dalit women suffer both gender and caste-based violence. The

UN Special Rapporteur on violence against women has noted that "*Dalit* women face targeted violence, even rape and murder, by the state actors and powerful members of the dominant castes used to inflict political lessons and crush dissent within the community." Gender inequality sanctified by religious and cultural norms subordinates women and reinforces the patriarchal order, allowing for violence against them to be carried out within their own homes and communities as well.

Dalit women face verbal, physical and sexual violence in the public and private domain. This includes being verbally and physically attacked for any number of reasons in public, e.g. when trying to access public resources or attempting to seek justice after another incident of violence. In the private domain *Dalit* women are assaulted for not being dutiful wives, not bearing children or male children specifically or not bringing enough dowries into the marriage. The reason for this is because of the process of imitation and the desire of being sanskritized like upper castes; low castes also follow their old traditional status practices like dowry system. *Dalit* women face violence from community members, complicit police personnel, their in-laws and their families. Between norms of female subjugation and cultural norms regarding the "natural" caste hierarchy, women are constantly assaulted and taken advantage of.

Further, due to their low socio-economic status, *Dalit* women are often the victims of trafficking and sexual exploitation. *Dalit* women's sexual and bodily integrity are threatened and violated, even from a young age. Due to the caste hierarchy, dominant caste men have a perceived right over *Dalit* women's bodies while gender inequality and subordination norms play an important role in the perpetuation of marital rape and in-caste sexual assault. *Dalit* women are considered to be available sexually to any dominant caste man. Additionally, the use of forced temple prostitution and trafficking are major concerns for young *Dalit* girls. Sexual exploitation of *Dalit* women is a common occurrence due to their low socio-economic status and dominant caste members take advantage of their power and authority over them.

Women's Access to Justice

Sanctioned impunity on behalf of offenders is a major issue in

India, and the police often deny or purposefully neglect and delay *Dalit* women's right to legal aid and justice. In a submission to the UN Commission on the Status of Women, three Indian NGOs reported that 86 per cent of women who were victims of violence in the three states surveyed were unable to gain entry into the legal system and their cases would not appear in any official figures. Further, in the cases that did make it into the legal system, there was only a 0.79 per cent conviction rate for cases of violence by non-*Dalits* against *Dalit* women.

There is a consistent pattern of delay in report filing and irregularities regarding criminal procedures, which leads to widespread impunity and creates serious barriers to justice for *Dalit* women. Impunity sends the message that gender and caste-based violence is tolerated and is thus perpetuated because there is no effective deterrence for offenders. Often in cases of rape, *Dalit* women are pressured to withdraw or settle, sometimes making a 'compromise' and receiving a small payment by dominant caste members or others in the community. Another tactic is for the accused or a dominant caste member to file a counter case and make a false accusation against the woman or her family. These cases are often more vigorously investigated than the original case lodged by the *Dalit* woman.

Conclusion

Indian democracy is full of contradictions and possibilities. The country has adopted for Uniform laws and its equal protection, but every time we get ashamed by new stories of humiliation, discrimination, atrocities etc. The weaker sections now are more powerful and assertive than before, but they always face paradoxes from the dominant sections of the society. So the problem of *Dalit* women has to be analysed within a three tier approach of caste, class and Gender.

REFERENCES

A 2010 Lenten Study compiled by the World Council of Churches, The World Student Christian Federation and the World YWCA.

Agrawal, S. (1999). *"Genocide of Women in Hinduism"*. Sudrastan Books, Jabalpur, India.

Atrocities against Dalit Women and Access to Justice—A Study by Evidence (2011), covering figures from 2005-2010.

Chakravarti, Uma. (2009). *Gendering Caste: Through a Feminist Lens*, Street Publications, Kolkata.

Geetha, V. (1992). "*Gender and Logic of Brahmanism: E.V. Ramaswamy Periyar and the Politics of the Female Body*', Paper presented at the Seminar on Women's Studies, IIAS: Shimla.

Guru, G. (1995). Dalit Women Talk Differently, *Economic and Political Weekly*, October 14-21, pp. 2548-49.

Mangubhai, Jayshree P. Aloysius Irudayamj, and Emma Sydenham (2009). *Dalit Women's Right to Political Participation in Rural Panchayati Raj—A Study of Gujarat and Tamil Nadu*,. IDEAS, Justitia et Pax, Equalinrights, 2009.

Manu (1920). *Manusmriti: The Laws of Manu with the Bhashya of Medhatithi*. Translated by Ganga Natha Jha. University of Calcutta, Calcutta, India.

Narula, S. (1999). "*Broken People: Caste Violence against India's Untouchables*", London. Human Rights Watch.

Rege, S. (1998). "*Dalit Women Talk Differently: A Critique of 'Difference' and towards a Dalit Feminist Standpoint Position*", 6(2) Vikalp Alternatives, Vikas Adhyayan Kendra, Mumbai.

The Annual Reports of University Grants Commission, New Delhi.

The National Commission for Scheduled Castes and Scheduled Tribes, Government of India.

Thind, G.S. (1995). "Our Indian Sub-Continent Heritage", Crosstown Press, LTD British Columbia, Canada.

http://www.dalitstan.org/books/

http://www.women.overcomingviolence.org

News Archives. http://www.ambedkar.org.

10

Powerlessness of Female Sexworkers in Relation to Condom Usage

A Socialist Feminist Analysis

Sudeshna Mukherjee and *Rashmi, C.K.*

This chapter proposes to understand the very essence of violation of health rights of Female Sexworkers within the ambit of their profession. The chapter projects the various internal and external factors that contribute towards manipulating the powers of female Sexworkers to negotiate safe sex and provides the feminist analysis of the same.

Bangalore has an estimate of 24300 Female Sexworkers IBBA (2006-2009) and HIV/AIDS reduction related programmes over the past decade has focused Female Sexworkers in its intervention strategies. The major shift in the health issues of Female Sexworkers emerged with the onset of these HIV/AIDS intervention programmes which considered 'Commercial Sex' as the primary driver of HIV. Thus, one of the three main strategies employed in HIV/AIDS prevention programmes to address HIV prevention among FSWs and their clients is promotion of safer sex behaviour through a peer mediated communications strategy, with particular focus on promotion of condom use.

Though Bangalore has seen decline in HIV prevalence among FSWs from 19.6 per cent to 10.8 per cent (ShajyIsac, B.M. Ramesh, *et al.*, 2015). The challenge still lies in the behavioural aspect of the Female Sexworkers (FSWs) and her clients to consistently and correctly use condoms in every sexual encounter. By interviewing 200 FSWs who have been part of this ongoing HIV intervention programme this chapter highlights the factors that control the power-relation between the FSW and the client and further disturbs the consistency pattern in condom usage among FSWs with their clients or partners.

The study is based on Feminist Methodology. Primary sources of information is collected through quantitative approach. Secondary sources of information collected from literature reviews, published and unpublished reports of previous studies etc. This study was initiated in collaboration with Society for People's Action for Development (SPAD)—an NGO and Vijaya Mahila Sanga (VMS)—a community based organization both involved in the HIV prevention programmes with FSWs in ZONE-2 area.

Study Design and Sampling

Sampling Universe

It is estimated that 24300 FSWs are living in Bangalore (Karnataka State AIDS Control Society, Mapping Exercise, Bangalore, 2004). Thereby following the city's administrative division into seven zones. The Sampling Universe includes Home based Female Sex Workers (FSWs) who solicited in the slums of Bangalore ZONE-2 area in Bangalore city (i.e. FSWs residing in the Slums of Kengeri, Ullalu Upanagara, Doddabasthi, Nayendanahalli, Gangondana-halli, Bapujinagar, Venkateshwara slum, Anandpuram, K.R. Market). An estimated 915 home based FSWs were identified in slums of Bangalore Zone 2 area by Society for People's Action for Development (SPAD)—an NGO and Vijaya Mahila Sangha (VMS)—a community based organization both involved in the HIV prevention programmes with FSWs in ZONE-2 area.

Using data from Integrated Biological and Behavioural Assessment (IBBA) among Karnataka Sexworkers, NACO typology predicts HIV risk. NACO typology takes into account both place of solicitation and place of sex to better captures the HIV risk variation experienced by women working in different settings. This extended typology distinguishes between women who solicit and have sex in brothels (brothel-to-brothel); women who solicit and have sex in their homes (home-to-home); and women who solicit in public places but have sex in various locations (street-to-home, street-to-rented-room, street-to-lodge, street-to-street).

Sampling Method

The sampling technique choosen for the study was Non-probability Purposive Sampling.

Non-probability sampling represents a valuable group of sampling techniques that can be used in research that follows *qualitative, mixed methods,* and even *quantitative research designs.* When following a *qualitative research design,* non-probability sampling techniques, such as *purposive sampling,* can provide researchers with strong *theoretical* reasons for their choice of units (or cases) to be included in their sample. Rather than using probabilistic methods (i.e., random selection) to generate a sample, non-probability sampling requires researchers to use their *subjective judgements,* drawing on *theory* (i.e., the academic literature) and *practice* (i.e. the experience of the researcher and the evolutionary nature of the research process). Unlike probability sampling, the goal is not to achieve *objectivity* in the selection of samples, or necessarily attempt to make generalizations (i.e., statistical inferences) from the sample being studied to the wider population of interest. Instead, researchers following a qualitative research design tend to be interested in the *intricacies* of the sample being studied (http://dissertation.laerd.com).

Hence Purposive Sampling method was adopted to choose the respondents for the study. A specific condition was imposed for selection of samples in Zone II area, i.e. the study mainly considered samples who were homebased FSWs under the intervention HIV intervention programme.

The typology of sexwork in these area is mainly home based. While other typologies were excluded because the major focus was on Home based sexworker who were difficult to be traced and identified for HIV interventions hence purposive sampling was considered.

Sample Size

The target sample size was 200 Home based FSWs from the slums of Bangalore Zone II area.

Tool Used Interview Schedules

A structured interview schedule was prepared and administered among all the respondents. Interview was choosen because the same questions needed to be asked to each interviewee in the same order so that the data collected could be quantified.

The schedule for the study consisted of—

1. Socio-Demographic characteristics, including age, age at sexual debut, marital status, literacy, source of income other than sex work and local status;
2. Sex work characteristics, including age at starting sex work, usual place of solicitation and sex client volume;
3. Condom use; including accessibility, usage consistency with various types of clients;
4. Condom use during Risk behaviour; and
5. Violence; includes physical and sexual.

Findings

The study considered respondents who came under the age group of 18-50 years.

The median age of the respondents interviewed was 30 years. 44 per cent of the respondents are illiterates, the maximum schooling they have attained is either up to 7th grade (22% respondents) or 10th grade (20% respondents).

The age of first sexual debute of 77 per cent of the respondents was lesser than 18 yrs. The probability of being HIV infected was approximately 0.75 times lower for FSW who had their sexual debut when they were older than 15 yrs. of age compared with under 15 yrs (B.M. Ramesh, S. Moses, R. Washington *et al.*, 2008: S35-S44).

Reasons for Getting into Sex work

- 67. 5 per cent FSWs got into Sex work purely due to their financial constraints of their family. 24 per cent due to desertion or separation (*see* Table 10.1).
- 32 per cent FSW respondents expressed that one or more of her family member is also in sex work (*see* Table 10.1).

Table 10.1: Reasons for Getting into Sex Work

Reasons for Getting into Sex Work	*FSWs %*
Trafficking	8.1
Cheated and lured by Unknown	7.6
Poor financial Condition of parents/ Husband and debt	67.5
Work place compulsion	1.5
Peer Influence	14.1
Left Destitute due to death of parents/husband	16.7
Left destitute due to separation/desertion	23.8

Note: Multiple choice.

Marital Status

The marital status of the respondents seems to be an indicator to the psychosocial and economic support they are dependent on. Although a good percentage of the respondents were married, the Table 10.2, indicates that there are 20.3 per cent FSWs are widowed and hence are psychologically and socially vulnerable. And comparatively higher percentage of FSWs are separated or deserted, from their husbands.

Table 10.2: Marital Status

Marital Status	*FSW %*
Unmarried	8.2
Married and currently living with husband	36.6
Widowed	20.3
Separated/deserted from husband	34.9

Out of the 63.4 per cent FSWs who fall under the categories of unmarried/widowed/separated/deserted. It was observed that these 47.2 per cent FSWs either had permanent clients or permanent partners.

Nature of Partners/Clients

The study came across two types of partner among the FSWs.

Firstly Permanent Visiting Client: They are men who were earlier occasional clients but over a period of time turned out to be more a frequent client. The FSW chooses this frequent client as her permanent client. Even if the FSW migrates the permanent clients will have contact with them. Their main characteristic is that they do not prefer to stay permanently with FSWs, but only wish to visit them so as to fulfil each others needs.

Secondly, Living partner/permanent partner: These are men who wish to or a FSW wishes to consider as permanent partners. The main characteristics of permanent partner is that they reside with the FSWs and most of the time provide social support. Some of them also provide economic and emotional support. The FSWs who have permanent partners express a sense of social security from neighbours and society.

Partner Status

From Table 10.3, it is evident comparatively higher percentage of FSWs have permanent visiting clients. And often these permanent visiting client are prone to STIs because of their mobility and sexual behaviour. Hence, it is evident that these FSWs are more at risk in contracting the STIs from these permanent visiting clients compared to permanent live-in partners.

Table 10.3: Status of the Partner

Partner Status	*FSW %*
Permanent visiting client	26.4
Living Partner/Permanent Partner	20.8

Reasons for Unhappiness in Husband and Partners Behaviour

Table 10.4 shows that the FSWs are less powerful in dealing with their partners/Husbands whims and fancies. It is also evident that FSWs face regular physical and sexual violence from their often alcoholic husbands/partners. These parasitic male partners thrive on the incomes of FSWs.

Client Volume: 64.9 per cent FSW respondents agreed that in a week they entertain more than 5 clients. Weekly client volume has direct relation to vulnerability to infections. 64.5 per cent earn Rs. 200 to Rs. 400 per client.

Table 10.4: Reasons for Feeling Unhappy about Husband Behaviour or Partner Behaviour

Reasons	*FSWs %*
Monetary dependency of Husband/Partner	23.4
Alcoholism of Husband/Partner	42.6
Regular Physical Violence	25.4
Forceful Sex (When least interested)	19.3
Debt for the sake of Husband/Partner	29.1

Note: Respondents have given more than one reason for their dissatisfaction with their current partners and husband.

Type of Clients

The study indicates majority of the clients of the FSWs belong to low socio-economic background and from high risk category. The social and economic status of the FSWs determines the type of client they choose. Moreover, earlier studies have proved that migrant labourers and lorry drivers are considered to be high risk categories vulnerable to STIs. So, Table 10.5 clearly indicates that the local social and economic status of the FSWs gives them no other choice rather to choose clients who also belong to similar social and economic background and who are in turn high risk categories by themselves.

Table 10.5: Type of Clients

Type of Clients	*FSWs %*
Migrant labourers (Coolie/construction workers/daily or weekly wage workers)	43.2
Lorry Drivers	22.4
Auto Driver/Car drivers	52.2
Hamali	7.1
Students	13.2
Officials and professional	32.9
Others (Unemployed, Self-employed etc.)	36.0

Note: Respondents have provided multiple answers from the above choices.

Methods of Contacting Clients

From Table 10.6 it is understood that majority of FSWs are more involved in soliciting alone or through broker or pimps. This way

Table 10.6: Methods of Contacting Clients

Method	*FSWs %*
Through referrals by friends/peers	39.5
Through phone contact	50.2
Through broker/Agent	30.0
By soliciting alone	34.5
By soliciting along with friends	17.8
Other	15.8

Note: Multiple choices are provided by the respondents

majority of the FSWs are not adapting safer meansto solicit clients, i.e. through friends, or known people. Hence they are open to risk and fall prey to exploitation, violence and transmission of diseases including AIDS.

Place of Entertaining Clients

Place of Entertainment also depicts how FSWs become vulnerable to the atrocities of clients. And in-turn decreases their power to negotiate safe sex.

Table 10.7: Place of Entertaining Clients

Place of Entertaining Client	*FSW %*
Own House	29.4
Friends House (by paying rent)	12.7
Friends House (without paying rent)	47.2
In rooms of Client	53.7
Lodge	34.4
Open isolated area behind bush	18.3
Vehical	8.1

Note: Multiple choices are provided by the respondents.

Majority of the FSWs involve with clients in the rooms of the clients, followed by temporary accommodation provided by co-sexworker in their own residing house (without paying rent) and in lodge. These are places where the condom negotiation is least possible because of time and space constraint and because the client is fully taking control of the situation. Clients are at more advantage in their own territory and the power of FSWs to negotiate condom usage in the territory of the client is less.

According to a study *"HIV among female Sexworkers in India"* by Ramesh and *et al.* 2005—"Vulnerability to HIV infection was also strongly associated with the organization of sexwork, including the place where an FSW solicits her clients."

Condom Use

24.9 per cent of the FSWs informed that they purchase condom from nearby shop/condom outlet. But for these FSW purchasing condom from a nearby outlet was the last option, especially when they entertain their clients in an open isolated area or in vehicles. Only 14.2 per cent of the FSWs expressed that they always carry condoms themselves. Majority of the FSWs, i.e. 66.4 per cent rely on the client to bring a condom. In such a situation the decision of using condoms is with the client and the probability of client to lure the FSW not to use condom could be high.

Table 10.8: Place of Procuring Condoms

Source/Place from where condom is availed	*FSWs %*
Always carry it with self	14.2
Client usually brings it along	66.4
Purchase from near by shop or condom outlet	24.9
Borrow it from peers	46.2
Availed at the place of entertaining clients	9.6
Any other	12.1

Note: Multiple choices are provided by the respondents.

Condom Negotiation

Table 10.9 indicates that almost half of the FSWs interviewed feel that it is impossible to negotiate condom usage with permanent

Table 10.9: Type of Client with Whom its Highly Imposible to Use Condoms

Client type (with whom condom negotiation is difficult)	*FSWs %*
Permanent clients	51.8
With clients who offer more money and insist not to use condoms	21.8
Police	4.1
Goondas	12.6
Any other client	28.4

Note: Multiple choices are provided by the respondents.

clients. The power of negotiation declines with clients who are in powerful profession. This is once again a misconception of the FSWs. More number of FSW are of the false opinion that those clients who are dressed officially (clean and neat) usually do not have STI and hence its not necessary to use condom with such clients.

Consistency in Condom Usage

Out of the last 10 sexual intercourses between the FSWs and clients about 35.5 per cent of the FSW used condoms all the time consistently. So the consistency rate of condom usage among the FSWs is low.

Possibility of not Using Condoms with Permanent Client

More FSWs feel powerless to negotiate condom usage with the permanent clients. 35.05 per cent of FSWs feel powerless to negotiate condom usage with the permanent clients.

Reasons for not Using Condoms

Table 10.10 indicates that the male power plays a role even in manipulating the FSWs behaviour to refraining condom usage.

61.9 per cent of the FSWs are in the habit of consuming alcohol during sexwork. Earlier studies had shown that alcohol consumption during sexual act effects condom usage and also leads to risky sexual behaviour. Alcohol consumption during sexual act will affect condom usage (i.e. improper application of condom leading to breakage of condoms or not using condoms at all).

Table 10.10: Reasons for Not Using Condoms

Reasons for not using Condoms	*FSWs %*
Client offered more money	17.8
Not aware of condoms	0.8
Don't know the place of availability	3.6
Clients insisted not to use condoms	30.0
Felt not necessary	9.1
Forced to have sex	3.5
Did not have sense of self because of alcohol consumption	14.7
Other reasons	20.5

36 per cent of FSWs faced physical violence from different perpetrators during the past one year period and 15 per cent FSWs faced violence from clients and partners.

13 per cent FSWs experienced sexual violence from occasional clients, regular clients, police, goondas and partners. Moreover it was also evident that FSWs who were subjected to extreme violence and it became highly impossible for them to negotiate condom usage during most of the occasions.

Socialist Feminist Analysis

According to a study *"HIV among female Sexworkers in India"* by Ramesh and *et al.*, 2005—"Vulnerability to HIV infection was also strongly associated with the organization of sexwork, including the place where an FSW solicits her clients". Since, HIV infection has direct relation to unprotected sex, it can be said that vulnerability of FSWs to HIV is the result of factors that interplay in manipulating the behaviour of Sexworkers towards condom usage. Socialist Feminism makes it clear that a Sexworker being a female and the social environment that she is into is playing a major role in oppressing her power to bargain for safe sex practice. The social factors that are analysed in this chapter are those in relation to the typology of the environment where the Female Sexworkers of Bangalore Zone II operate and the type of clients they entertain and also the situations such as physical and sexual violence they encounter. These factors makes it hard for a sexworker to negotiate condom usage. And since it is the only means of her earning, the chapter tries to analyse how the Female Sexworker's own belief as a person in a degraded profession along with the misconceptions that arise while bargaining her fee with different clients is oppressing her powers to exercise her right to health.

Conclusion

Hence the women's own beliefs, myths and misconception, their low level of confidence and capacity, lack of ability to bargain collectively, and their unquestioning acceptance of established power and social structures contribute to the internal factors. Violence harassment afflicted upon the women but in relation to

Female Sexworkers—Exploitation, discrimination, domination are the causes for violence. Sexual harassment is a tool for suppressing women. Moreover, the numbers in the table clearly indicates that FSWs can become easy targets of sexual harassment. Thus discrimination caused by the social structure within which the sex industry operates accounts to the external factors.

Thus, the internal and external power factors control condom negotiation. It is important to design and implement programmes for understanding of right issues in relation to power, security, access to control over material resources, social participation and sense of community.

Suggestions

FSWs seem to reflect a host of other risk factors such as current age, sex client volume, age at sexual debut, as well as age at starting sex work. These variables have been found in other studies to be important predictors contributing to health risk among FSWs (Plummer FA, Nagelkerke, *et al.*, 1991: S169-S176).

FSWs are considerably at higher risk in relation to their sexual health. The stage of lifecycle at which a woman enters sexwork and the way the sexwork is organized. These variations in the structure of sexwork clearly have implications. Feminist analysis on these risk factors can be taken up in detail for future studies.

REFERENCES

Bradley, J. *et al.* (2009). *'Assessing reported condom use among female sex workers in southern India through examination of condom availability,* An International peer-reviewed journal for health professionals in all areas of sexual health, Open Access, 18 November, 2009.

Excerpts from an interview with writer and activist Leela Sampige; (Joint Director—KASAPS) during book release titled 'Buddanillada Amrapalli'—Rashmi Shrikanth, Protect Rights of Sexworkers: September 24, 2014.

Integrated Behavioural and Biological Assessments—IBBA (2006-2009)

Isac, Shajy, B.M Ramesh, S. Rajaram, Reynold Washington, Janet E. Bradley, Sushena Reza-Paul, Tara S. Beattie, Michel Alary, James F. Blanchard, Stephen Moses (2015). *Changes in HIV and syphilis.*

Prevalence among female sex workers from three serial cross-sectional survey sin Karnataka state, South India' Downloaded from http://bmjopen.bmj.com on October 5, 2015—Published by group.bmj.com

Plummer, F.A., Nagelkerke, N.J.D., Moses, S., Ndinya-Achola, J.O., Bwayo, J., Ngugi, E. (1991). The importance of core groups in the epidemiology and control of HIV-1 infection. *AIDS*; 5 (Suppl. 1): S169-S176.

Ramesh, B.M., S. Moses, R. Washington *et al.* (2008). "Determinants of HIV prevalence among female sexworkers in four south Indian states: analysis of cross-sectional surveys in twenty-three districts," *AIDS*, vol. 22, no. 5, pp. S35-S44, 2008.

Sjoerd, M. Euser *et al.* (2012). "Pragati: An empowerment programme for female sex workers in Bangalore, India", *Global Health Action,* India, pp. 1-10.

Ties, B.J. (2005). Weir, S.S. Integrating demographic and epidemiological approaches to research on HIV/AIDS: the proximate-determinants framework. *J Infect Dis*; 191 (Suppl. 1): S61-S67.

11

Gender Disparity and Economic Empowerment of Women in Relation with Flower Vending Business

A Primary Survey Analysis with Special Reference to Kolaghat Flower Market of Purba Medinipur District, West Bengal

Labani Dey and *S.A.H. Moinuddin*

Vending as a part of informal sector's employment act as a vital ingredient in surviving life. In this backdrop, the present chapter seeks to analyse the gender disparity and economic empowerment of women flower vendors in Kolaghat flower market of Purba Medinipur district. The analysis of the study is based on primary survey through scheduled questionnaire. From our study we found that there prevails disparity in terms of economic status across gender. Economic status comprises three major components—income, savings and debt status. Male flower vendors are better off than the female in terms of these components. Our study also reveals that though there is gender disparity but the female flower vendors get a pathway to empowered themselves through this job. Our study confirms that the women flower vendors are empowered in terms of their economic decision making.

Introduction

The informal sector is the lifeline for many people in less industrialized nations, particularly in semi-urban areas, in terms of employment provision. An important feature of the informal sector in India is vending. Vendors are those traders who operate from the streets or occupy legally distributed stalls at a given area selling different goods (Mitullah, 2003; Cohen *et al.*, 2000). These range from traders in fruit and vegetables, to those selling crafted products, traditional herbs, pottery, sculpture, fabrics, cosmetics, flowers, kitchen-ware etc. The market for vendors is largely the pedestrians. In a few cases, especially when they have done business in one spot for a long time, customer relations develop, thereby expanding the market beyond the general pedestrians.

Some vendors look for customers in offices, homes and beyond the urban areas where they are based. This (practice) is quite dominant among those who have invested substantially in street trade, especially those who use trucks, pick-ups and bicycles. Such vendors trade in cooked food, fruits, vegetables and clothes. Overall, however, high transport costs and low profits prohibit street traders from accessing alternative and better markets (Mitullah, 2003; Motala, 2002; Cohen *et al.*, 2000). Market relations are usually mutual, except in cases where there is intense competition among street vendors. Poor location of business, low purchasing power among customers and unreliability of customers who take goods on credit also affects the market. In addition, low levels of professionalism due to low technical education among vendors and low access to modern information communication technologies on productivity information hinders their performance in business marketing (Motala, 2002).

In this regard, flower vending turns as an important source of Income for the women where the spatial conditions are in favour of floriculture. Though there exists gender earnings differentials in which women usually receive lower wage/income than man in the same occupation, and this is true across all occupations. However, there is a little research on gender difference in work performance and empowerment issues and this is true across all occupations. Some recent studies in West Bengal (Sarker, 2004; Sarker and Chakrabarti, 2005; 2006; 2011; 2013) lends credence to the fact that the trade market of flower crop in West Bengal, which employ a large section of women marketing agents in all types of flower markets in West Bengal, receive annual net real income compared with their male counterpart, though all the reasons of lower income for the former is not tested directly.

The present study is undertaken to assess the gender disparity based on economic status as well as the economic empowerment of women through vending of flowers in Kolaghat flower market of Purba Midnapore district; West Bengal, where a large section of women are engaged in vending flowers. This study seems to be important in that successful entrepreneurship for rural women in floriculture, who are almost still in the informal sector and remain invisible in the official national statistics, is very crucial to the agricultural development of the economy in general and empowerment of women in agriculture in particular.

Brief Survey of Literature

"Gender equality and women's empowerment is one of the eight United Nations Millennium Development Goals" (UN, 2008). According to United Nations Secretary-General Ban Ki-moon, women are not just the target of special measures to promote development. They are also the driving force to overcome poverty, reduce hunger, fight illiteracy, heal the sick, prevent the spread of disease and promote stability (UN, 2008).

Gender equality and women's empowerment are considered to be a desirable by product of human development. Therefore, to achieve these goals, it is essential to close the gender equality and empowerment gaps in education, employment, and political participation (Kabeer, 2005).

One of the areas of disparity between males and females is related to the difference in their employment status which is manifested by occupational segregation, gender-based wage gaps, and women's disproportionate representation in informal employment, unpaid work and higher unemployment rates (UNFPA, 2005).

As women in developing countries have low status in the community, the activities they perform tend to be valued less; and women's low status is also perpetuated through the low value placed on their activities (March *et al.*, 1999).

Therefore, empowerment of Women is a necessity for the very development of a society, since it enhances both the quality and the quantity of human resources available for development. There are several vital reasons for evaluating, promoting and monitoring the level of women's empowerment. Enhancing women's status and their empowerment can play a decisive role in the success of many development programmes and bring about positive social changes. Women's empowerment is necessary for ensuring not just their own health and welfare but also the well-being of the entire household. They are the primary means by which social norms are transmitted to their children and thus are placed in a critical position to inculcate attitudes in favour of gender equality among their children and households. Additionally, if they have egalitarian attitudes towards gender, this orientation enhances their decisions to allocate empowerment resources to their children without gender discrimination. From this perspective, an individual woman's empowerment could trigger the empowerment process at the household, community and societal levels and thus challenge prevailing patriarchal gender norms. Discrimination against women is also a violation of their basic human rights as it hampers women's abilities to realize their full potential.

Gender inequality is rooted in social stratification based on the roles and responsibilities assigned to men and women and the differential valuation of these roles. Thus women's position and degree of empowerment is determined by the ways that gender identities, gender roles and gender relations are conceived at the family, household, community and societal levels. The differential valuation of the tasks performed by men and women remains the root cause of attitudes that result in differential investment in men and women with regard to such development forces as secular education, skill formation, and income generating activities. The crux of the problem in gender relations lies in the fact that gender roles, rights and obligations are not just different but they are highly unequal. In almost every sphere of human functioning in India, the roles defined for women are subordinated to those defined for males, the rights for women are fewer or less emancipating than those of men, and women's obligations are more limiting than those of men, resulting in gender disparity at every level, cutting across all types of class and caste powerlessness (Malhotra *et al.*, 2002).

Batliwala (1995) and Schüler and Hashemi (1993), have stated that the process of empowerment has to begin in a woman's individual consciousness and later has to be externalized through greater autonomy, physical mobility, remunerated labour, and a strong role in the household. The beliefs, thought, conscience and attitudes may or can contribute to fulfilling women and men's moral, ethical and spiritual needs, or alternatively, these factors may hamper the realization of women's full potential in society.

However, any form of extremism may have a negative impact on women and can lead to violence and discrimination (United Nations, 1995b). The beliefs about appropriate roles and activities of men and women and the behaviours and status resulting from these beliefs can be altered if women are intrinsically empowered in an egalitarian way.

In this context, focus is not only on eliminating the constraints on women's access to resources such as education, information, and income, but also on women's decision-making roles, their economic self-reliance, their mobility, and their legal rights to equal treatment, inheritance and protection against all forms of discrimination (Germain and Kyte, 1995; United Nations, 1995). The three important components of empowerment included in much of the literature are "resources", "agency" and "achievements", though different authors have used different terms with respect to these three components. Resources are enabling factors that are catalysts for empowerment and not the empowerment per se. The second concept, agency, is the heart of many conceptualizations of empowerment. It encompasses the ability to formulate strategic choices, to gain autonomy, and to control resources and decisions that affect important life outcomes. Achievements are identified as the well-being outcomes that women experience as a result of access to resources and agency.

The 2009 World Survey on the Role of Women in Development (UN DESA, 2009) verifies that there are positive multiplier effects for overall social and economic development when women, in the same extent as men, access economic and financial resources. This is seen through poverty reduction, children's increased welfare and increased household efficiency. Robust evidence shows that women's access to resources has a stronger impact on child survival, welfare and education, than when men have access to similar resources (UN DESA, 2009: 7).

Amartya Sen (2000: 201) states that when women participate in economic activities the society as a whole benefits. Social benefits are provided through women's enhanced status and independence. Women are empowered through the reduction of gender bias in household decisions and have the possibility to generate income and affect the reduction of mortality and fertility rates in the society.

Women can be empowered in many ways; socially, economically, politically and legally. This thesis focuses on household dynamics, individual characteristics and gender-related constraints, when it comes to social and economic empowerment. In the discussion on women's empowerment, gender equality and gender equity is terminology which is interrelated. Equality implies the condition or quality of being equal and equity is the equality of rights (Webster's Dictionary, 2010). In contrast to other terms, women's empowerment relates to a process; a progression from one state to another. In addition, empowerment includes agency, in which women themselves are actors in the empowerment process. They must not only be able to make a decision, but be aware of their rights to make it. Women's empowerment encompasses a complexity in comparison to other disadvantaged groups. Women make up half of the world's population, and form a cross-cutting group that overlaps all other groups in society. Compared to other disadvantaged or socially excluded groups, the household and family relations play a central part in women's disempowerment (Boender *et al.*, 2002: 5).

The main objectives of our study are:

(i) To assess gender disparity based on economic status of the flower vendors in Kolaghat flower market.
(ii) To examine the economic empowerment status associated with women flower vendors.

The rest of the study can be summarized as: Section 2 deals with the methodological issues. Section 3 analyses the results obtained. Lastly, Section 4 deals with summary and conclusion of our study.

The present study based on primary survey collected from Kolaghat flower market of Purba Medinipur District.

Now, to assess economic status of flower vendor, cross sectional sampling survey method is used through scheduled questionnaire. In drawing of samples, the simple random sampling without replacement technique has been used in our study.

A simple random sample from finite population is a sample selected such that each possible sample combination has equal probability of being chosen. It is also called unrestricted random sampling. Now, in simple random sampling without replacement technique the population elements can enter the sample only once, i.e. the units once selected is not returned to the population before the next draw.

In this backdrop, 80 women as well as 80 men flower vendors are surveyed through our scheduled questionnaire in Kolaghat flower market.

In our study, gender disparities in terms of economic status is measured through income, saving and debt status of the flower vendors. On the other hand, economic empowerment of women comprises ability to participate in formulating and executing decision regarding spending the money, final say on large household purchases, final say on daily household purchase and lastly the decision about their health care.

Results and Discussion

'Economic empowerment is about making markets work for women (at the policy level) and empowering women to compete in markets (at the agency level)' (World Bank, 2006: 4).

Now, those women who enter into the market with minimum level of investment must rely on their physical labour and luck to meet their daily needs. They are seldom in a position to negotiate the price of their flower products or opt for leisure if they do not receive their asking price. Those with considerable investment in the flower vending business, on the other hand, are not only better able to determine the price at which they will engage in market transactions and to take advantage of any new opportunities that may emerge, they are also in a position to close off such opportunities to less fortunate groups. In this regard, we find that the male flower vendors are more secured in this business and also they utilized more opportunities in the market than the women flower vendors.

In this backdrop, in our study, to analyse the gender disparities in relation with economic status mainly comprises three aspects: First; monthly income of the flower vendors, second; saving pattern of the vendors and third; debt status of the vendors in the flower market.

Status of Monthly Level of Income

We found that the women who work in the flower vending business earn less than the male flower vendors. It can be said that the women generally earn less than their husbands who are also engaged in this business and sometimes when she plays the role of family head (in case of divorcee or widow women) they have to fight for their subsistence. Though in both cases, these women gets significance in the family as they are earning members too. Working in the vending business generally adds more workload on women since they also have to perform the household chores. Nevertheless, it helps them to gain respect and provide them scope for active participation in the process of decision making.

In this regard, although the data on the income through flower vending business cannot perfectly reflect their original standard of living structure but it can help us to understand the basic livelihood status of the women flower vendors as well as the male flower vendors.

Table 11.1: Monthly Level of Income of the Flower Vendor in Kolaghat Flower Market

Monthly Level of Income (in INR)	*Women*	*Men*	*Total*
< 1000	1	4	5
1001-4999	23	9	32
5000-9999	34	17	51
10000-14999	13	29	42
15000-19999	6	13	19
>20000	3	8	11
Total	**80**	**80**	**160**

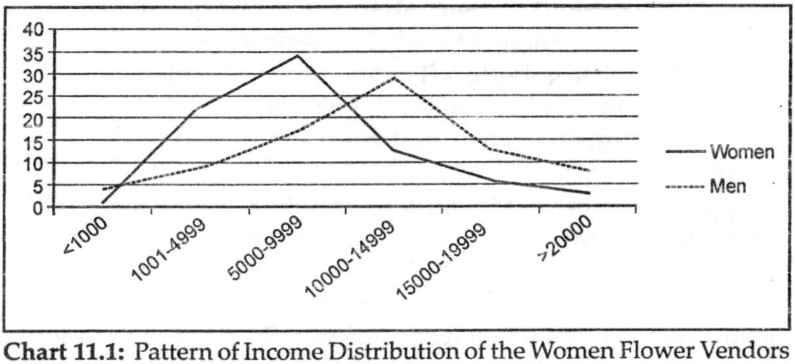

Chart 11.1: Pattern of Income Distribution of the Women Flower Vendors

From, the above Tables 11.1 as well as from the diagram on income distribution status, we found that around 71.25 per cent women flower vendors income fall within the range of 1000 to 9999 rupees, whereas, only 32.5 per cent of male flower vendors' income comes under this head. We also found that the 16.25 per cent women earning in the range of 10000 to 14999 rupees, while, 36.25 per cent male flower vendors', which is also the majority, come under this head. Now, only 11.25 per cent women earn more than rupees 15 thousand while 26.25 per cent male flower vendors income falls in this category.

Therefore, we can say that, there is a clear gender disparity in the income distribution between the flower vendors. Though, for most of the women the subsistence level of income to survive in the sphere of life may be the reason that attracts them to this business. Their earnings though not sufficient but it helps them to live a subsistent standard of living.

Status of Monthly Savings

From our survey, we found that savings act as a vital ingredient of investment in the flower vending business. Table 11.2, depicts that 41.25 per cent of women flower vendors saves less than 500 rupees per month. 32.5 per cent women flower vendors save rupees 500 to 999 rupees per month while only 26.25 per cent of women flower vendors saves more than one thousand rupees. We found that the respondents in our study whenever they earn some extra amount through this business they try to save it. In this regard, they also use their savings for future precautions. Generally, maximum women flower vendors save their money in rural banks and post office.

Table 11.2: Saving Pattern of the Flower Vendors in Kolaghat Flower Market

Monthly Level of Saving (in INR)	*Women*	*Men*	*Total*
< 500	33	2	35
500-999	26	13	39
1000-1499	12	26	38
1500-1999	5	21	26
2000-2499	2	12	14
>2500	2	6	8
Total	**80**	**80**	**160**

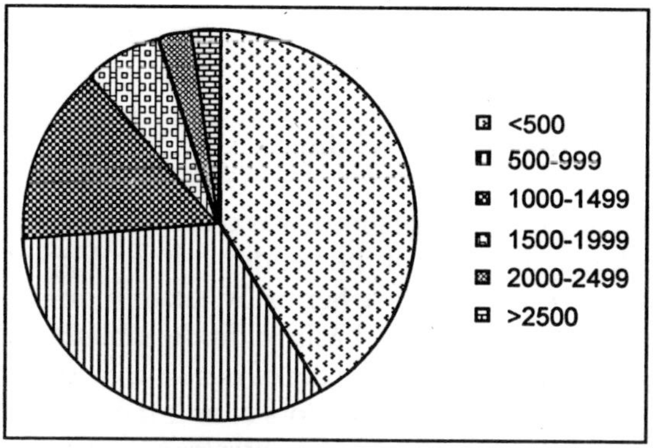

Chart 11.2: Monthly Saving Pattern of the Women Flower Vendors

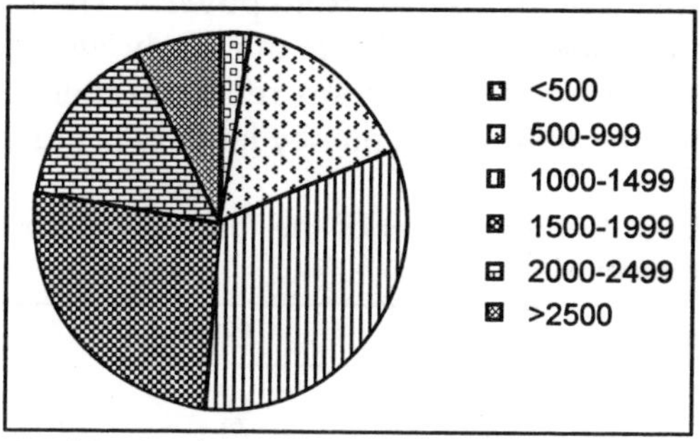

Chart 11.3: Monthly Saving Pattern of the Male Flower Vendors

Again, by considering Table 11.2, we found that only 2.5 per cent male flower vendors save less than 500 rupees per month. We found that majority of the male vendors (58.75 per cent) savings ranges between 1000-1999 rupees. This is quite significant outcome with respect to increased income level of the male flower vendors when compared to women. Therefore, in the saving pattern we also found the disparity between male and female.

In this regard, in the Kolaghat flower market, the high percentage of flower vendors using their own savings seems to be possible because their incomes have increased rapidly since they got the security of vending zone. We may say that, in the Kolaghat flower market of Purba Medinipur district, it is possible that their turnover was fairly high that's why they could invest from their own savings. However, in all cases, the flower vendors were not really large scale business persons. So it was possible to refinance their micro business through their own savings. It also helps them in being psychologically secure.

Debt Status of the Flower Vendors

As far as finance for their business was concerned, in the Kolaghat flower market, a majority of the vendors either dipped into their own savings as mentioned earlier or by taken money on interest from money lenders on daily basis to do their business.

Though the alternative sources of funding carry high rates of interest, which often ruin the vendors or as is the case of the female vendors in the flower markets, they live from hand to mouth and not able to alleviate themselves from poverty. The most frequent source is from moneylenders. From our study, we found that, the majority of the vendors of both sex relied on their own sources. We found that the reliance on money lenders is much lower.

Table 11.3: Debt Burden Status of the Flower Vendors in Kolaghat Flower Market

Debt Status	*Women*	*Men*	*Total*
Yes	12	7	19
No	68	73	141
Total	**80**	**80**	**160**

From the above Table, we found that only 15 per cent women flower vendors rely on the debt-based flower vending business whereas only 8.75 per cent male flower vendors rely on this. Therefore, we can conclude, though majority of the flower vendors doesn't rely on debt based flower vending but as a marginalised group, majority of the women flower vendors are empowered and self-reliance as they does not prefer borrowing to make their business but the part of women who debt to operate their business is also greater than the male debtor.

Response over the Economic Decision by the Women Flower Vendors

Participation in economic decision-making in their family refers to the extent of women's flower vendor ability to participate in formulating and executing decision regarding spending the money, final say on large household purchases, final say on daily household purchase and lasty the decision about their health care.

Data cited in Table 11.4 show around 42.5 per cent respondents in our study have the right to spent their income as per their choice.

Table 11.4: Decision about the Spending of the Money Income

Decision Maker	*Kolaghat Flower Market*
Self	34
Husband	18
Self and Husband	26
Others member of the Family	2
Total	**80**

From our study, it is also revealed that the decision about the money spending sometimes influenced by their husband as 32.5 per cent women flower vendor makes decision about their spending with their husband. It is worth noting from our study that 22.5 per cent women flower vendors handover their income to their husband. Around 2.5 per cent women flower vendors rely on their family members, e.g. son, daughter, in-laws, to take decision about the spending their money. This is due to the dependency of the respondents on their family members due to old-age or due to psychological dependency on the family members.

From Table 11.5, we seeks to study the decision making pattern about the final say on large household purchases. From our study we found that generally husband takes the decision about the large household purchases as in our study we found 38.75 per cent respondent says that their husband takes the decision on it. Therefore, it appears that women employment does not necessarily change power equation within the family. Though 33.75 per cent women flower vendors can take their own decision regarding this. It is quite interesting to find that 23.75 per cent women flower vendors take joint decision with their husband. Therefore, we can say that around 57.5 per cent women have the power to decide large household purchases either fully or partially.

Table 11.5: Final say on Large Household Purchase

Decision Maker	*Kolaghat Flower Market*
Self	27
Husband	31
Self and Husband	19
Other members of the Family	3
Total	**80**

Table 11.6, shows around 77.5 per cent women has the final say on daily household purchases. This is quite interesting findings as because in this decision making process which plays the most powerful role. This is may be due to the reason that most of the women flower vendors restrain both the vending business as well as the household chores. Only 13.75 per cent women flower vendor make decision jointly on it with their husband. While only 5 per cent cases husband take the soul decision about it.

Table 11.6: Final say on Daily Household Purchase

Decision Maker	*Kolaghat Flower Market*
Self	62
Husband	4
Self and Husband	11
Others member of the Family	3
Total	**80**

Table 11.7: Decision about the Health Care

Decision Maker	*Kolaghat Flower Market*
Self	48
Self and Husband	23
With others member of the Family	7
Someone else	2
Total	**80**

Lastly the decision about their health care is presented in Table 11.7. The respondent in our study shows that they can take care of themselves on health issues as around 85 per cent respondent say that they can go to the nearest rural hospitals or to the doctors independently in minor or medium health issues. But in case of big health issues they may have to rely on their husband or family members. 28.75 per cent respondents say that the health issues of them are take care by both of their husband and them while 8.75 per cent says that the decision about their health care is taken care off by their family members.

Conclusion

The lives of women have been positively changing through the participation in flower vending business in Kolaghat flower market of Purba Medinipur district, but, there is a clear gender differences prevails.

In general, women's high self-worth to decision is a sign of growing consciousness. Over time, women have been increasingly involved in decision making. We found that the women do well in regulating and controlling their lives as the majority of the women's decision is at the highest satisfactory level.

Thus, we may say that the women related to flower vending business in Kolaghat flower market of Purba Medinipur district achieve and increase their level of empowerment through this job.

The main factor affecting their level of empowerment is mainly the power to make economic decisions in their life as well as in the society.

Though, when we compared there economic status with the male flower vendors then we find that women are lagging behind in respect with earnings and savings. Our study postulates that the average income of the majority of the women is far lower than the average income of the male. Now, as income is low, thus, the overall savings made by the women is also low when we compared that with the male. Therefore, using the results of this study, to overcome the gender disparity, we recommend certain steps to improve the power practice of women.

(a) Women have perceptions about their rights and abilities. Sustained support from the state and society is necessary to motivate their perceptions.

(b) Involvement in income-generating activities should be expanded because of its supportive role in women power practice and because it has a correlation with their empowerment. Support to women should be provided in the form of income-related activities to make them active stakeholders of the economy.

(c) A good working environment, as well as reliable traffic and security systems, should be provided to encourage the mobility of women related to the flower vending business.

REFERENCES

Ali, R. (2013). *Empowerment beyond resistance: Cultural ways of negotiating power relations*. Women's Studies International Forum (in press). Retrieved on July 24, 2013 from http://dx.doi.org/10.1016/j.wsif.2013.05.019.

Alsop, R., and Heinsohn, N. (2005). Measuring empowerment in practice: Structuring analysis and framing indicators. *World Bank Policy Research Working Paper 3510*. Washington, DC: World Bank.

Anand, S., and Sen, A.K. (1994). Human Development Index: Methodology and Measurement. *Human Development Report Office Occasional Paper No. 12*. New York: United Nations Development Programme.

Balk, D. (1994). Individual and community aspects of women's status and fertility in rural Bangladesh. *Population Studies,* 48 (1): 21-45.

Balk, D. (1997). Defying gender norms in rural Bangladesh: A social demographic analysis. *Population Studies,* 51: 153-172.

Cohen, M. and Garrett, J.L. (2010) The food price crisis and urban food (in) security. *Environment and Urbanization,* 22 (2), pp. 467-482.

Dixon M. (1993). *Population Policy and Women's Rights: Transforming Reproductive Choice*. Connecticut: Praeger.

Dixon, R. (1978). *Rural Woman at Work*. Baltimore: The Johns Hopkins University Press.

Haregewoin, C., Emebet, M. (2003). *Towards Gender equality in Ethiopia. A Profile of Gender Relations*. Swedish International Development Cooperation Agency.

Hindin, M.J. (2000). Women's power and anthropometric status in Zimbabwe. *Soc.Sci.Med,* 51: 1517-1528.

Hindin, M.J. (2005). Women's Autonomy, Status, and Nutrition in Zimbabwe, Zambia, and Malawi. In: Kishor, S. (ed.) *A Focus on Gender: Collected Papers on Gender Using DHS Data*. Calverton, Maryland, USA: ORC Macro.

Hirut, T. (2004). Violence Against Women in Ethiopia: A Strong Case of Civil Society Concern. In: Chowdhury, S., Wais, A., and Kahsai Wolde

Giorgis (Eds.) *Civil Society in Ethiopia: Reflections on Realities and Perspectives of Hope*. African-Asian Studies Promotion Association.

Jejeebhoy, S.J. (2000). Women's autonomy in rural India: Its dimensions, determinants and the influence of context. In Harriet B. and Gita Sen Presser, *Women's empowerment and demographic processes*. New York: Oxford University Press.

Jejeebhoy, S.J., Sathar, Z.A. (2001). Women's autonomy in India and Pakistan: The influence of religion and region. *Population and Development Review*, 27(4): 687-712.

Joshi, S.T. (1999). *Women and Development—The changing scenario*. New Delhi: Mittal Publications.

Kabeer, N. (1998). "Money Can't Buy Me Love? Re-evaluating Gender, Credit and Empowerment in Rural Bangladesh", *IDS Discussion Paper 363*.

Kabeer, N. (2001). "Reflections on the Measurement of Women's Empowerment in Discussing Women's Empowerment: Theory and Practice", *SIDA Studies No. 3*. Stockholm: Swedish International Development Cooperation Agency.

Kabira, W.M., Masinjila, M. (1997). *ABC of Gender Analysis*. Forum for African Women Educationalists, Nairobi, Kenya.

Keller, B. and D.C. Mbwewe (1991). "Policy and Planning for the Empowerment of Zambia's Women Farmers", *Canadian Journal of Development Studies* 12(1): 75-88.

Kennedy, G., Nantel, G., Brouwer, I.D., and Kok, F.J. (2006). Does living in an urban environment confer advantages for childhood nutritional status? Analysis of disparities in nutritional status by wealth and residence in Angola, Central African Republic and Senegal. *Public health nutrition*, 9(02), 187-193.

Kishor S. (2000). Empowerment of women in Egypt and links to the survival and health of their infants. In Harriet B. and Gita Sen Presser, *Women's empowerment and demographic processes*, New York: Oxford University Press.

Kishor, S. (ed.) (2005). *A Focus on Gender: Collected Papers on Gender Using DHS Data*. Calverton, Maryland, USA: ORC Macro.

Kritz, M.M., Makinwa-Adebusoye P., Gurak, D.T. (2000). The role of gender context in shaping reproductive behaviour in Nigeria. In: Harriet B. and Gita Sen Presser, Women's empowerment and demographic processes, New York: Oxford University Press.

March, C., Smyth, I. and Mukhopadhyay, M. (1999). *A Guide to Gender Analysis Frameworks*. Oxfam Print Unit.

Mason K.O. (1986). The status of women: conceptual and methodological issues in demographic studies. *Sociological Forum*, 1(2): 284-300.

Mitullah, W.V. (2003). Street Vending in African Cities: Synthesis of Empirical Findings from Kenya, Cote d'Ivoire, Ghana, Zimbabwe,

Uganda and South Africa. Washington DC, World Bank—*A Contribution to World Development Report on Investment Climate and Informal Enterprises.*

Mukuria, A., Aboulfia, C. and Themme, A. (2005). The Context of Women's Health: Results from the Demographic and Health Surveys, 1994-2001. *Comparative Reports No. 11*. Calverton, Maryland: ORC Macro.

Rugh, A. (1984). *Family in contemporary Egypt*. Syracuse, New York: Syracuse University Press.

Schuler, S.R. and Hashemi, S.M. (1994). Credit programs, women's empowerment, and contraceptive use in rural Bangladesh. *Studies in Family Planning*, 25(2): 65-76.

Sen, S. and Batliwala, S. (2000). Empowering women for reproductive rights. In: Harriet B. and Gita Sen Presser, *Women's empowerment and demographic processes*. New York: Oxford University Press.

UN (1995). Beijing Declaration and Platform for Action, 1995. *The Fourth World Conference on Women, 4-15 September 1995*, Beijing, China. Retrieved on July 26, 2013 from http://www.un.org/womenwatch/daw/beijing/pdf/BDPfA%20E.pdf

UN (2009). 2009 world survey on the role of women in development, women's control over economic resources and access to financial resources, including microfinance. New York: Department of Economic and Social Affairs Division for the Advancement of Women, United Nations. Retrieved on February 6, 2014 from http://www.un.org/womenwatch/daw/public/WorldSurvey2009.pdf

UNDP (2010). Human Development Report, 2010.

UNDP (United Nations Development Programme). (2005). *Human Development Reports 2005*. New York and Oxford: Oxford University.

UNFPA (2005). *The State of World Population. The Promise of Equality: Gender Equity, Reproductive Health and the Millennium Development Goals*.http://www.unfpa.org/swp/2005/presskit/factsheete/facts_gender.htm

UNFPA (2005a). *Culture matters to development: It is the "how" and not the "why" and the "what"*. New York: UNFPA, UN Population Fund. Retrieved on August 13, 2013 from http://www.unfpa.org/public/News/pid/2469

World Economic Forum (2005). *Women's Empowerment: Measuring the Global Gender Gap*, Switzerland.

12

Trends in Feminist Thought

With Special Reference to Indian Feminism

Rajni Bala

The Webster's Dictionary defines the term 'feminism' as (a) the principle that women should have political rights equal to those of men, (b) the movement to win such rights for women is called Feminism.

The word 'feminism', however, must be understood in the broadest sense as referring to an intense awareness of identity as a woman, and interest in feminine problems. Its meaning should not be restricted to the advocacy of women's rights. According to the feminist doctrine, the subjugation of women is a central fact of history, a key to most of our social and psychological disorders. But the word 'feminism' has picked up so many connotations that it seems to have no precise meaning, and what it stands for may be easily misunderstood.

The early feminists did not use the term 'Feminism'. Had they given any name to themselves, possibly it would have been something like 'defenders' or 'advocates' of women. Their immediate aim was to oppose mistreatment of women. By exposing ideology and opposing the prejudice and narrowness it fostered, they stood for a general conception of humanity.

Feminists view the world as being unequal on the basis of gender. They wish to see the gender gap and the idea that men are superior to women decreased or even abolished. So feminist philosophy works on the belief that women, like all human beings, have the right to be born, to have the same opportunities to live and work using fully their human potential. They should not be discriminated against because of their gender and that they should be able to make their own choices on how to live their lives. The inequalities against which the feminists protest are—legal, economic and the social restrictions on the basic rights of women—which have existed throughout history and in all the civilizations.

The Feminist Movement

The feminist movement started almost two centuries ago when in Europe, some women dared to resist male oppression, prominent of these women are Hildegard of Bingen in 11th century, Julian of Norwich in the 15th century and Margery Kempe in the 16th century. By the late 16th century increasing number of women started showing their concern for women issues more consistently and more aggressively.

The First-Wave Feminism

What historians refer to as "first-wave feminism" arguably began in the late 18th century with the publication of Mary Wollstonecraft's *Vindication of the Rights of Woman* (1792), and ended with the ratification of the Twentieth Amendment of the U.S. Constitution, which protected a woman's right to vote. First-wave feminism was concerned primarily with establishing, as a point of policy, that women are human beings and should not be treated like property.

The two best known 19th century arguments for women's rights were written by men, though in both cases the authors—William Thompson and John Stuart Mill—acknowledge the influence and inspiration of their wives. In this time the right to vote became central to feminist demands, as denial of representation in legislature was a clear message of second class citizenship. It was seen as important both symbolically and practically, but winning the vote proved a complicated struggle, one that lasted for decades. By the 1890s, women's sense of disparity and injustice increased sharply. They pointed out that men who were poor and barely literate had been given the vote, while well educated women, who pay taxes were still excluded from full citizenship. By the early 1870s, a few women were taking the idea of 'no taxation without representation' literally and were refusing to pay taxes. Emily Davison sacrificed herself for this cause for winning the right to vote for women, by throwing herself under the king's horse on Derby Day in 1913. Ultimately in 1918, women above the age of 30 were given the vote and in March 1928, they finally won it on equal terms with men.

Second-Wave Feminism

Second-wave feminism emerged after the Second World War in several countries. One of the most remarkable French writers, Simone de Beauvoir gave many important explorations of one woman's experience through her writings including four volumes of her autobiography and several novels. In her book 'The Second Sex' (1949), she argues that woman has been denied full humanity, denied the human rights to create, to invest, to go beyond mere living to find a meaning for life in projects of ever widening scope. Her writings offered the first sustainable analysis of the construction of women as 'other'. She stated that woman appears to man essentially as a sexual being. She is forced to take a secondary position in relation to man. She also pointed out that a woman is not biologically feminine but she is made so by constant cultural conditioning. "One is not born, but rather becomes a woman. No biological, psychological or economic fate determines the figure that the female presents in society. It is civilization as a whole that produces the creature which is described as feminine' (qtd. in Walter 98).

Third-Wave Feminism

Rebecca Walker, a 23-year-old, African-American woman born in Jackson, Mississippi, coined the term "third-wave feminism" in a 1992 essay. Walker is in many ways a living symbol of the way that second-wave feminism has historically failed to incorporate the voices of many young women, non-heterosexual women, and women of colour (http://civilliberty.about.com/od/gender sexuality). Both first-wave and second-wave feminism represented movements that existed alongside, and at times in tension with, civil rights movements for people of colour—a slight majority of whom happen to be women. But the struggle always seemed to be for the rights of white women, as represented by the women's liberation movement, and black men, as represented by the civil rights movement. Both movements, at times, could have been legitimately accused of relegating women of colour to asterisk status.

Calls for the fourth wave feminism have also started with the demise of Hillary Clinton's campaign in early 2008 and the blatant, repugnant sexism that so publicly followed her bid for the presidency. Perhaps the most notable call was Amanda Fortini's *New York Magazine* article *"The Feminist Reawakening: Hillary Clinton and the Fourth Wave,"* which appeared in April 2008 and documented a revival of feminist feeling (http:/nymag.com/news/ features).

Third World Feminism

The feminist movement is basically attached to the European countries so there is always a major issue of the applicability of feminist though in other parts of the earth especially in the Third World countries. More than political and economic equality between the sexes, there are problems of class, race, ethnicity and even honour killings, dowry, *sati pratha* and domestic violence in case of countries like India and Pakistan. The main objection of Third World feminists to the first world feminists is that they have been ignoring issues like race, ethnicity and class pertaining to women of Third World countries. The Western feminists assume hegemonic stance and view the Third World women as inferior, illiterate, conservative and submissive, while women in the first world are perceived as educated, modern and free. There are emerging tribal studies also in the Third World feminists which includes Chandra Talpade Mohanty, Kumkum Sangari, Kumare Jayawardena, Susie Tharu, Sara Suleri, Fatima Mernissi and many others. These feminists have dealt with problems of women in Third World countries, particularly South Asia. These feminists have paid attention to issues like dowry deaths, honour killings, resurgence of *Sati*, practice of *Watta-Satta* and many more such issues. Related to the rise of feminism among women of colour is the area of post-colonial studies. Among its most prominent feminist voices is that of Gayatri Chakravorty Spivak. She examines the effects of political independence upon sub-altern or sub proletarian women, in the Third World countries. Spivak makes clear the major differences among feminists depending upon class and political structure (Guerin, 2006). According to Spivak's highly polemical essay, '*Can the Subaltern Speak?*' (1988), everything that a subaltern requires to speak her mind like—the language, the texts, the channels are implicated in colonial politics.

Ideological Pinning of Feminism

Several distinct ideologies can be discerned within feminism. All ideologies stem from one fact, that women require freedom and equality but all these viewpoints differ on the philosophic questions about the nature of freedom and equality, mainly four ideologies can be outlined, which are as under:

The Conservative View

The conservative view is that the differential treatment of women, as a group, is not unjust. They admit that some individual women do suffer hardships, but this suffering is not a part of the systematic social oppression. The conservatives are fully convinced of the inherent unequal abilities of men and women, all of them give emphasis that one of the main tasks of the state is to ensure that the individual performs his or her proper social functions. They argue that social differentiation between the sexes is not unjust, since justice not only allows but requires us to treat unequal unequally.

The Liberal View

This school of thought in feminism takes liberation of women as the most important agenda of the feminist movement. Liberal feminists want women should have freedom to determine their own social roles and equality with men as much as possible. This view advocates every kind of liberty for all the members of the society. In this world every individual is engaged in constant competition with every other in order to maximise her or his own-self interests and the function of the state is to make sure all these competitions to be fair and without any biases. It should give equal opportunities to all its members irrespective of their class, race or sex. So, 'equality of opportunities to women' is the main agenda of these liberal feminists.

Classical Marxist Feminism

For Marxist, oppression is the chief characteristic of a society, where, a small class of individuals owns the means of production and hence is able to dominate the lives of the majority who are forced to sell their labour power in order to survive. So, the classical Marxist feminist views the oppression of women as historically and currently a direct result of the private property.

According to Marxist feminists, the special oppression of women results primarily from their traditional position in the family. This excludes women from participation in public production and relegates them to domestic work in the private world of home. From its inception to the present day, monogamous marriage was designed to perpetuate the consolidation of wealth in the hands of a few, and these few are men.

Radical Feminism

This school of thought is a recent attempt to create a new conceptual model for understanding many different forms of social oppression in terms of the basic concept of sexual oppression. This new view in feminism devised by writers like Atkinson and Firestone rejects the liberal claim that the basis of women's oppression consists in their lack of political and civil rights. They even deny the classical Marxist view that basically women are oppressed because they live in a class society and the root cause for their exploitation is the system of capitalism. The radicals claim that the roots of women's oppression are biological and their subjection lies in the fact that as a result of the weakness caused by childbearing, women become dependent on men for physical survival. So long before the institution of private property and its corollary, class oppression, physical subjection of women by men was historically the basic form of oppression. The power relationships that develop within the biological family provide a model for understanding all other types of oppression such as racism and class society. The battle against capitalism and against racism is subsidiary to the more fundamental struggle against sexism.

Thus, all these schools of thought work on the 'consciousness of victimization of women'. To apprehend oneself as victim is to be aware of an alien and hostile force which is responsible for the blatantly unjust treatment of women. This hostile power is, for some feminists, 'society', or the 'system', for others, it is, simply, 'men'. This consciousness also brings a sense of solidarity with other victims. In sum, feminist consciousness is the consciousness of being radically alienated from her world and often divided against herself. It perceives woman as a being who sees herself as victim and whose victimization determines her being-in-the-world as resistance, wariness and suspicion. Woman is immersed in social reality that exhibits to her an aspect of malevolent ambiguity. She is an outsider to her society, to many of the people she loves, and to the still unemancipated elements in her own personality.

Recent Trends in Feminist Thought

The present day feminist thought encompasses a moral vision and emerges as a holistic, anti-materialistic and life affirming philosophy. Toril Moi (1988) has used the term 'post-feminism' to cover the different configurations of feminism. The modern feminist theorists believe that strictly speaking, feminism is an impossible position and as Toril Moi (1988) says, "In a non-sexist, non-patriarchal society, feminism will no longer exist". By 'modern feminism' she means, "movement from the point of view of, by and for women". Thus, today feminism must be viewed as a rapidly developing major critical ideology or system of ideas in its own right. The concept incorporates a broad spectrum of ideas and possesses an international scope.

The present day feminism though seeks to destroy masculinist hierarchy but not sexual dualism. It is necessary pro-woman, but this does not mean that it has to be anti-man. This acts as a rebalancing factor between women and men of the social, political and economic power within a given society. It is viewed as a humanistic philosophy, which prefers the word 'transformation' rather than 'revolution'. So, the modern feminism emerges as a thought system, a point of view to reorganize the world realities, a positivist holistic approach to life, a step towards sanity in human relationship and perhaps the only mode for preservation of human existence on this planet.

Though feminism has uplifted the status of women by fighting against social and political inequalities, yet there are many challenges especially in the Third World countries. Bell Hooks, one of the most eminent and articulate spokespersons of black feminist thought, has pointed out that black feminists are concerned about economic survival and ethnic and racial discrimination as well as sexism. She finds faults with the main stream white women's movement for failing to speak to these issues (Rice, 2002). Feminism has to combat sexism in the form of deep rooted local beliefs and practices, to do away with class, caste, religion and ethnic biases. Issues like genital mutilation of African countries and stoning as a legal punishment in Iran have to be handled urgently.

Indian Feminism

The history of the Indian woman is one that has witnessed some grave assaults. In fact, *Sati*, child marriages, segregation of widows and intermittent sexual exploitation still exist in certain parts of the country. Women in every sphere of their lives face opposition and criticism. Constantly, they are reminded that their status is below that of a man. Human rights and equality are constitutionally provided, but when it comes to the territory of home or for that matter work, these rights cease to exist and protect a woman's integrity and body. The woman has always existed on the margins of human existence, assuming gender-specific roles in the periphery of a circle that centers on the man. Compared to the West, women empowerment and independence in India is seen in a different light. Historical circumstances and values in India make women's issues different from the western feminist rhetoric. The idea of women as "powerful" is accommodated into patriarchal culture through religion. This has retained visibility in all sections of society; by providing women with traditional "cultural spaces". Another consideration is that whereas in the West the notion of "self" rests in competitive individualism where people are described as "born free yet everywhere in chains", by contrast in India the individual is usually considered to be just one part of the larger social collective, dependent for its survival upon cooperation and self-denial for the greater good. The most striking feature of Indian Feminism is that women are called to emancipate and liberate themselves in the sphere of their relations and families. Indian feminists do not seek mere rebellion; rather, the search is for a system where they can be who they want to be, without anybody raising their eyebrows. Many women believe that Indian feminism is relevant only to the rural, poor or uneducated and cannot be explained on the same lines as Western feminism, as it is located in a different cultural consciousness and seems about someone else. And its hard to get worked up over other people's fights. To be more relevant in India, feminism has to be more current context, more communicative, more inclusive and less judgmental. That is why, if, Western feminism has concentrated on the issues like, fight for vote, equal pay for equal work, equality of opportunities, reproductive rights, and against female feticide, sexual harassment, domestic violence etc., Indian feminism is taking up many new issues like equal rights at work, maternity policies lack of awareness domestic violence, abuse issues, divorce laws, marital rape, inequality in terms of housekeeping and parenting street sexual harassment, sexual harassment at the workplace, rape, control over contraception, unwanted pregnancy, abortion etc. The feminist movement, though subjected to scrutiny and criticism, seeks to uplift women in their entirety rather than in fragments.

Though India has emerged as an independent nation, the cause of female emancipation still seems to be in its nascent stages. Although many leaders of feminism have been women, not all women are feminists and not all feminists are women. Some feminists argue that men should not take positions of leadership in the movement, but most accept or seek the support of men Sahitya Akademi award-winning writer Shashi Deshpande opined that perhaps it is not easy for men to associate themselves with feminism, since the very word carries connotations of 'women' (*Times of India,* 22 July, 2001), http://timesofindia.indiatimes.com/cityhyderabad. Ashok Khosla, director of the NGO Development Alternatives who has worked for many years in areas of women's welfare, offers a male perspective. "A number of Indian feminists have a hands-on, problem-solving kind of approach," he says. "And they are practical about what they want". Shanta Gokhale, journalist and author, says that more men's groups like MAWA (Men Against Women Abuse) are needed. "In any case, the success of the feminist movement is essentially because issues have been tackled from with in the community rather than imposed from the outside" (*Outlook*, December 20, 1995).

When Action India, a women's organisation, travelled to Saharanpur to raise awareness about equal rights, they realised the limits of their own awareness. Rajbala, an elderly resident of the area, posed a question to which Action India had no answer. "Equality? Equality with whom? Equality for what? Will my stomach be filled with equality? I don't want equality with my man. I want equality with you, you who have cars and send your children to English-speaking schools." In a situation of extreme poverty, trying to secure equal rights for women is meaningless. Where men and women are both demeaned by poverty, why ask for equal status with a man? "Irresponsible conscience-raising," says Karlekar, "is, I think, a thing of the past. The point is, after exhorting women to revolt, where will they go? Can we offer jobs? Or shelter? There is a need look at the entire picture from all angels" (http://www.dishin.org/reports).

The issue of abortion, a vital demand for Western feminists—that it should be treated as a choice to be made only by the pregnant woman—in India is fraught with complications. The practice of amniocentesis and sex determination ultra-sound tests means that abortion is often not a choice but is imposed by social pressures. Thus a pro-abortion crusade can often play into the hands of forces inimical to the feminist agenda.

Indian feminism in the 90s is trying to reach a stage where it draws on indigenous traditions of emancipation for its growth. As such it works within the confines of Indian society instead of trying to overthrow the system from the outside. So, religion is no longer denied, but communalism is combated; the family is not sought to be destroyed, only reformed from patriarchy; equality with men is no longer seen as the ultimate prescription for freedom; and abortion and contraception are no longer absolute imperatives for the health of Indian women. Ideology still divides, but not as crucially as in the West where perhaps it would be unthinkable for left-wing and conservative women to work together. In India the Seven Sisters—a group of seven women's organisations with differing political affiliations—have worked together to secure law reform, press for petitions and function as a pressure group on the government. Says feminist lawyer Lotika Sarkar: "We have nothing to do with the West. We are very down to earth. And as far as women's issues are concerned, there is a united front" (http://www.outlookindia.com/articles).

So, there is a new identity-in-the-making for Indian feminism in the decade when the movement has come into its own as a pressure lobby on the government. It is hybrid, yet rooted; Western in theory but indigenous in practice; rationalist in inspiration but at the same time forced to come to terms with some aspects of Indian custom and tradition.

REFERENCES

Betty, Friedan (1974). *The Feminine Mystique.* New York: Norton.

Carden, Maren Lockwood (1974). *The New Feminist Movement.* New York: Russell Sage Foundation

Estelle B. Freedman (2002). *No Turning back: The History of Feminism and the future of Women.* New York: Ballantine Books.

Germaine, Greer (1997). *The Female Eunuch,* London: Paladin.

Goodman, Lizbeth Ed. (1996). *Literature and Gender.* London: Routledge.

Heyman, G.D., Legare, C.H. (2004). Children beliefs about Genders Differences in Academic and Social Domains. *Sex Roles,* 50: 227-36.

Kang, Manpreet (2008). *Seeking a Female Identity: Adrienne Rich and Anne Sexton.* New Delhi: Prestige Books.

Mill, John Stuart (1989). *The Subjection of Women* (First Published 1869). 12th Printing, Cambridge: The M.I.T. Press.

Millet, Kate (1970). *Sexual Politics.* New York: Doubleday, p. 39.

Moi, Toril (2006). *Sexual/Textual Politics: Feminist Literary Theory,* 2nd ed. London: Routledge.

Richards, Janet Radcliff (1982). *The Skeptical Feminist: A Philosophical Inquiry.* London: Penguin.

Walters, Margaret (2005). *Feminism: A Very Short Introduction.* New Delhi: Oxford University Press.

Wollstonecraft, Mary (1985). *Vindication of the Rights of Women.* Reprinted, Penguin Classics, London: Penguin Books Ltd.

Woolf, Virginia (1992). *A Room for One's Own and Three Guineas,* Oxford World's Classics. New York: Oxford University Press.

http://www.education.nic.in

http://www.hinduonnet.com/mag/2008/03/09/stories

http://www.indianexpress.com

http://www.indianexpress.com.news

http://www.outlookindia.com/articles.asp

http://www.outlookindia.com/printarticle

http://www.tribuneindia.com

http://www.unesco.org

Index